Slow Cooking

igloobooks

Published in 2014
by Igloo Books Ltd
Cottage Farm
Sywell
Northants
NN6 0BJ
www.igloobooks.com

Food photography and recipe development: PhotoCuisine UK
Front and back cover images © PhotoCuisine UK

GUA006 0714
2 4 6 8 10 9 7 5 3 1
ISBN: 978-1-78343-478-7

Printed and manufactured in China

P42

P92

P160

Contents

P88

SOUPS & BROTHS 10

MEAT..40

FISH 104

STEWS & TAGINES 118

PUDDINGS 172

BAKES 206

SOUPS & BROTHS

SERVES

6

Seafood ragu

PREPARATION TIME: 15 MINUTES | COOKING TIME: 4 HOURS 15 MINUTES

INGREDIENTS

2 tbsp olive oil

1 onion, finely chopped

1 celery stick, finely chopped

1 carrot, finely chopped

4 cloves of garlic, finely chopped

800 g / 1 lb 12 ½ oz / 4 cups ripe
     tomatoes, chopped

300 g / 10 ½ oz / 2 cups baby squid,
     cleaned

450 g / 1 lb live mussels, scrubbed

300 g / 10 ½ oz / 2 cups raw king
     prawns

1 monkfish tail, boned and cut into
     chunks

salt and black pepper

GARNISH

2 tbsp flat leaf parsley, chopped

- Heat the oil in a frying pan and fry the onion, celery, carrot and garlic for 5 minutes without colouring.

- Tip the mixture into a slow cooker and stir in the tomatoes and squid, then cover and cook on medium for 4 hours.

- While the tomato mix is cooking, heat a large saucepan over the hob, then tip in the mussels and 3 tbsp of water. Cover and cook for 5 minutes or until the mussels have all opened. Tip the mussels into a sieve-lined bowl to collect the juices, then pick out the mussel meat and discard the shells.

- Stir the mussels and their juices into the tomatoes along with the prawns and monkfish. Cover and cook for another 15 minutes, then season to taste with salt and pepper and serve garnished with parsley.

SERVES

4

Poached chicken with spices

PREPARATION TIME: 15 MINUTES | COOKING TIME: 6 HOURS

INGREDIENTS

1.5 kg / 3 lb 5 oz oven-ready chicken
3 star anise
30 g / 1 oz piece of fresh root ginger,
    sliced
2 lemongrass stalks, bruised
1 bulb of garlic, halved horizontally
2 mild red chillies (chilies), sliced
75 ml / 2 ½ fl. oz / ⅓ cup shaoxing rice
    wine
75 ml / 2 ½ fl. oz / ⅓ cup dark soy
    sauce
3 spring onions (scallions), sliced
steamed rice, pak choi and chilli
    (chili) sauce to serve

- Lay the chicken in a slow cooker and surround with the star anise, ginger, lemongrass, garlic and chillies.

- Pour over the rice wine and soy sauce, then add enough cold water to cover the chicken by 2.5 cm (1 in). Cover the slow cooker and cook on low for 3 hours or until a temperature probe reads 75°C / 167F when inserted into the thickest part of the chicken. Stir the spring onions into the broth.

- Carve the chicken and serve with the broth spooned over and some steamed rice, pak choi and chilli sauce on the side.

SERVES

6

Chicken and barley broth

PREPARATION TIME: 15 MINUTES | COOKING TIME: 6 HOURS

INGREDIENTS

1 chicken carcass
2 tbsp olive oil
2 leeks, thinly sliced
2 cloves of garlic, crushed
100 g / 3 ½ oz / ½ cup pearl barley
½ head of broccoli, diced
½ hispi cabbage, shredded
salt and black pepper

- Put the chicken carcass in a slow cooker, breaking it into pieces if it is too large, then pour over enough cold water to cover.

- Cover and cook on low for 4 hours.

- Towards the end of the cooking time, heat the oil in a frying pan, then fry the leeks and garlic for 5 minutes without colouring.

- Remove and discard the chicken bones, then stir the leeks and barley into the stock. Cook on medium for 1 hour 30 minutes. Stir in the broccoli and cabbage and cook for a further 30 minutes.

- Season to taste with salt and pepper, then ladle into warm bowls to serve.

SERVES

4

Ham hock pot au feu

PREPARATION TIME: **10 MINUTES** | COOKING TIME: **6 HOURS**

INGREDIENTS

1 large ham hock
2 small onions, peeled
2 leeks, cut into short lengths
4 small carrots, peeled
2 bay leaves
½ tsp black peppercorns

- Put all of the ingredients in a slow cooker and pour over enough water to cover by 2.5 cm (2 in).
- Cover and cook on medium for 6 hours. Shred the ham off the bone and serve with the vegetables and cooking liquor.

SERVES

6

Carrot and squash soup

PREPARATION TIME: 20 MINUTES | COOKING TIME: 4 HOURS

INGREDIENTS

1 butternut squash, peeled, deseeded
   and cut into chunks
2 large carrots, peeled and cut into
   chunks
1 onion, finely chopped
2 cloves of garlic, finely chopped
1 tsp ground coriander (cilantro)
1 litre / 1 pint 15 fl. oz / 4 cups
   vegetable stock

GARNISH

6 tbsp soft goats' cheese
1 tbsp chives, chopped
1 tbsp coriander (cilantro) leaves,
   chopped
salt and black pepper

- Mix the squash and carrots with the onion, garlic and ground coriander in a slow cooker, then pour over the stock and season with salt and pepper.

- Cover the slow cooker and cook on high for 4 hours. Use a stick blender to puree the soup until smooth, then check the seasoning and adjust with salt and pepper.

- Ladle the soup into 6 warm bowls and top each one with a spoonful of goats' cheese and a sprinkle of herbs.

SERVES

4

Japanese prawn and noodle soup

PREPARATION TIME: 20 MINUTES | COOKING TIME: 2 HOURS 10 MINUTES

INGREDIENTS

300 g / 10 ½ oz / 2 cups raw king
   prawns
15 g / ½ oz piece of kombu
4 tbsp dried bonito flakes
200 g / 7 oz / 2 cups fresh rice noodles

GARNISH

2 spring onions (scallions), thinly
   sliced
2 mild red chillies (chilies), thinly
   sliced
2 tbsp coriander (cilantro) leaves

- Peel the prawns and put the heads and shells in a slow cooker. Pour in 1 litre of water, then cover and cook on medium for 2 hours.

- Stir in the kombu and bonito flakes, then cover and cook for 5 minutes.

- Strain the stock, then return it to the pan and stir in the noodles and prawns. Cover and cook for 3 minutes or until the prawns just turn opaque.

- Ladle the soup into warm bowls and garnish with spring onion, chilli and coriander.

SERVES

4

Mushroom soup

PREPARATION TIME: 15 MINUTES | COOKING TIME: 3 HOURS 30 MINUTES

INGREDIENTS

2 tbsp butter
1 leek, finely chopped
2 cloves of garlic, crushed
300 g / 10 ½ oz / 4 cups mushrooms,
    sliced
1 litre / 1 pint 15 fl. oz / 4 cups
    vegetable stock
100 ml / 3 ½ fl. oz / ½ cup double
    (heavy) cream
salt and black pepper

GARNISH

1 punnet of Enoki mushrooms
2 tbsp olive oil

- Heat the butter in a frying pan, then add the leek and garlic and cook without colouring for 5 minutes. Stir in the mushrooms and cook for 5 more minutes, then scrape the mixture into a slow cooker and stir in the stock.

- Cover the slow cooker and cook on low for 3 hours.

- Stir in the cream, then use a stick blender to puree the soup, leaving a few pieces of mushroom whole.

- Heat the oil in a small pan and gently fry the Enoki mushrooms until turning gold, then remove from the heat and reserve for the garnish.

- Season to taste with salt and pepper, then ladle into warm bowls and serve sprinkled with the Enoki mushrooms.

SERVES

4

Prawn and rice noodle broth

PREPARATION TIME: 15 MINUTES | COOKING TIME: 2 HOURS 15 MINUTES

INGREDIENTS

300 g / 10 ½ oz / 2 cups raw king
   prawns
3 tbsp dried black fungus
2 tbsp green Thai curry paste
1 red chilli (chili), sliced
1 tbsp fish sauce
1 tsp caster (superfine) sugar
200 g / 7 oz / 1 cup fresh rice
   vermicelli
100 g / 3 ½ oz / ¾ cup sugar snap peas

- Peel the prawns, leaving the tails intact, then put the heads and shells in a slow cooker with the fungus. Pour in 1 litre of water, then cover and cook on medium for 2 hours.

- Strain the stock, then return it to the pan with the fungus, discarding the heads and shells.

- Turn the heat to high and stir in the curry paste, chilli, fish sauce and caster sugar. Taste the broth and adjust with extra fish sauce or sugar accordingly.

- Add the noodles and sugar snaps to the pan, then cover and cook for 5 minutes. Add the prawns then cover and cook for 2 minutes or until they are just opaque. Ladle into bowls and serve.

SERVES

4

French onion soup

PREPARATION TIME: **10 MINUTES** | COOKING TIME: **7 HOURS**

INGREDIENTS

2 tbsp butter
3 onions, quartered and sliced
2 cloves of garlic, sliced
1 tbsp balsamic vinegar
1 tbsp runny honey
1 tbsp plain (all purpose) flour
125 ml/ 4 ½ fl. oz / ½ cup dark ale
1 litre / 1 pint 15 fl. oz / 4 cups
    vegetable stock
salt and black pepper

- Put the butter in a slow cooker and cook on high until it melts. Stir in the onions, garlic, balsamic and honey and season well with salt and pepper. Cover and cook on high for 1 hour, stirring every 15 minutes.

- Stir in the flour, then gradually incorporate the ale and stock, stirring as you go to eliminate any lumps. Cover and cook on low for 6 hours.

- Taste the soup for seasoning and adjust with salt and pepper, then ladle into warm bowls and serve.

SERVES

4

Chicken and celeriac stew

PREPARATION TIME: 15 MINUTES | COOKING TIME: 4 HOURS

INGREDIENTS

2 tbsp olive oil
450 g / 1 lb / 2 cups chicken breast,
    cubed
8 spring onions (scallions)
½ celeriac, peeled and julienned
2 cloves of garlic, crushed
1 lemon, juiced and zest pared into
    thin strips
600 ml / 1 pint / 2 ½ cups chicken
    stock
salt and black pepper

- Heat the oil in a frying pan and sear the chicken pieces all over. Transfer the chicken to a slow cooker with a slotted spoon.

- Reserve the green parts of the spring onions, then chop the rest and add them to the chicken with the celeriac, garlic and lemon zest.

- Pour over the stock, then cover and cook on low for 4 hours.

- Add lemon juice, salt and pepper to taste, then chop the spring onion greens and sprinkle them over the top.

SERVES

6

Bean and buckwheat broth

PREPARATION TIME: 25 MINUTES | COOKING TIME: 6-8 HOURS

INGREDIENTS

150 g / 5 ½ oz / 1 cup dried haricot
   beans, soaked overnight
150 g / 5 ½ oz / 1 cup dried kidney
   beans, soaked overnight
100 g / 3 ½ oz / ½ cup buckwheat
1 onion, quartered and sliced
2 bay leaves
4 tomatoes, quartered
150 g / 5 ½ oz / ¾ cup home-cooked
   ham, shredded (optional)

GARNISH

a few sprigs of flat leaf parsley
salt and black pepper

- Drain the beans from their soaking water and put them in a large saucepan of cold water. Bring to the boil and cook for 10 minutes, then drain well.

- Mix the beans with the buckwheat, onion and bay leaves in a slow cooker. Pour over enough boiling water to cover everything by 10 cm (4 in), then cook on low for 4 hours.

- Stir in the tomatoes and ham, if using, and cook for a further 2–4 hours or until the beans are tender, but still holding their shape.

- Season the broth to taste with salt and pepper, then stir in the parsley and serve.

SERVES

4

Leek, potato and bacon soup with pesto

PREPARATION TIME: 25 MINUTES | COOKING TIME: 6 HOURS

INGREDIENTS

1 ham bone
2 leeks, finely chopped
450 g / 1 lb / 3 cups potatoes, peeled
    and cubed
2 cloves of garlic, crushed
8 rashers back bacon
100 ml / 3 ½ fl. oz / ½ cup double
    (heavy) cream
2 tbsp pesto

GARNISH

a few sprigs of flat leaf parsley
salt and black pepper

- Put the ham bone in a slow cooker and pour over enough cold water to cover.

- Cover and cook on low for 4 hours. Remove and discard the bone, then stir in the leeks, potato and garlic. Cover and cook on medium for 2 hours.

- Towards the end of the cooking time, grill the bacon for 2 minutes on each side or until crisp, then slice it thinly.

- Puree the soup until smooth with a stick blender, then season to taste with salt and pepper.

- Ladle the soup into warm bowls and spoon a little pesto onto each. Sprinkle with bacon and garnish with parsley.

SERVES

6

Squash and apple soup

PREPARATION TIME: 10 MINUTES | COOKING TIME: 4 HOURS

INGREDIENTS

1 large butternut squash, peeled
  deseeded and diced
3 eating apples, cored and diced
1 onion, finely chopped
2 cloves of garlic, finely chopped
1 tsp ground caraway
1 litre / 1 pint 15 fl. oz / 4 cups
  vegetable stock
rye bread to serve
salt and black pepper

- Mix the squash with the apple, onion, garlic and
  caraway in a slow cooker, then pour over the stock
  and season with salt and pepper.

- Cover the slow cooker and cook on high for 4 hours.
  Use a potato masher to break down the squash into a
  puree, leaving some pieces of apple and squash whole.

- Ladle the soup into warm bowls and serve with rye
  bread.

SERVES

6

Chorizo and lentil soup

PREPARATION TIME: 5 MINUTES | COOKING TIME: 2 HOURS 30 MINUTES

INGREDIENTS

2 tbsp olive oil
225 g / 8 oz chorizo ring, sliced
1 onion, finely chopped
1 celery stick, sliced
2 cloves of garlic, crushed
400 g / 14 oz / 3 ¼ cups red lentils
1.2 litres / 2 pint / 5 cups vegetable
    stock
1 bay leaf
6 cherry tomatoes, halved
salt and black pepper

- Heat the oil in a large frying pan and fry the chorizo slices for 1 minute on each side. Transfer to a slow cooker and stir in the rest of the ingredients, except for the tomatoes.

- Cover and cook on high for 2 hours, then stir in the tomatoes and cook for 30 minutes.

- Taste the soup for seasoning and adjust with salt and pepper, then ladle into warm bowls and serve.

MEAT

SERVES

4

Chicken and butternut Colombo

PREPARATION TIME: 1 HOUR | COOKING TIME: 6 HOURS

INGREDIENTS

4 skinless chicken thighs, cut into
   chunks
½ butternut squash, peeled and cut
   into chunks
½ aubergine (eggplant), cubed
6 spring onions (scallions), chopped
2 cloves of garlic, finely chopped
2 cm (1 in) piece ginger, finely
   chopped
a few sprigs of thyme
2 tbsp Colombo seasoning or mild
   curry powder
400 ml / 14 fl. oz / 1 ⅔ cups chicken
   stock
200 ml / 7 fl. oz / ¾ cup light coconut
   milk
1 lime, juiced
salt and black pepper

- Mix the chicken, squash, aubergine, spring onions, garlic, ginger and thyme together in a slow cooker. Sprinkle over the Colombo seasoning and leave to marinate for 1 hour.

- Pour in the stock and coconut milk then cover and cook on medium for 6 hours, stirring occasionally.

- Stir in the lime juice and season to taste with salt and pepper before serving.

SERVES

4

Chicken with morels

PREPARATION TIME: 15 MINUTES | COOKING TIME: 4 HOURS

INGREDIENTS

2 tbsp butter

4 chicken breasts

2 shallots, finely chopped

2 cloves of garlic, finely chopped

1 bay leaf

50 g / 1 ¾ oz / ⅔ cup dried morels

600 ml / 1 pint / 2 ½ cups chicken
    stock

300 ml / 10 ½ fl. oz / 1 ¼ cups double
    (heavy) cream

tagliatelle, fried lardons and chopped
    chives to serve

salt and black pepper

GARNISH

cayenne pepper

- Heat the butter in a large frying pan and sear
  the chicken breasts on both sides. Transfer the
  chicken to a slow cooker and stir in the rest of the
  ingredients.

- Cover and cook on low for 4 hours.

- Taste the sauce for seasoning and adjust with salt
  and black pepper. Serve with tagliatelle tossed with
  fried lardons and chopped chives. Sprinkle with a
  little cayenne pepper.

SERVES

4

Beef in red wine
with shallots

PREPARATION TIME: 20 MINUTES | COOKING TIME: 6 HOURS

INGREDIENTS

450 g / 1 lb / 3 cups chuck steak, cut
  into large chunks
2 tbsp plain (all purpose) flour
2 tbsp olive oil
6 large shallots, halved
500 ml / 17 ½ fl. oz / 2 cups red wine
2 bay leaves
mashed potato to serve
salt and black pepper

GARNISH

flat leaf parsley

- Season the beef with salt and pepper and dust the pieces with flour to coat. Heat the oil in a large frying pan and sear the beef in batches on all sides. Remove the beef from the pan, then colour the cut side of the shallots.

- Transfer the beef and shallots to a slow cooker, tuck in the bay leaves and pour over the wine. Season well with salt and pepper.

- Put the lid on the slow cooker and cook on low for 6 hours, stirring every 2 hours. Garnish with parsley and serve with mashed potato.

SERVES

4

Pot-roasted paupiettes of veal with baby onions

PREPARATION TIME: 15 MINUTES | COOKING TIME: 1 HOUR 30 MINUTES

INGREDIENTS

4 good quality pork sausages, skinned
4 veal escallops
2 tbsp olive oil
450 g / 1 lb / ⅔ cups baby onions, peeled
1 bay leaf
150 ml / 5 ½ fl. oz / ⅔ cup dry white wine
150 ml / 5 ½ fl. oz / ⅔ cup veal stock
1 tbsp concentrated tomato puree
1 tbsp runny honey
1 tbsp white wine vinegar
salt and black pepper

• Preheat the oven to 180°C (160°C fan) / 350F / gas 4.

• Put a quarter of the sausage meat on top of each escallop, then gather up the sides into a cushion shape and tie securely with string.

• Heat the oil in a frying pan and sear the paupiettes on all sides.

• Transfer the paupiettes to a cast iron casserole dish and stir in the rest of the ingredients.

• Cover the pan and cook in the oven for 1 hour 30 minutes. Season to taste with salt and pepper before serving.

SERVES

4

Slow-baked Spanish chicken

PREPARATION TIME: **15 MINUTES** | COOKING TIME: **1 HOURS 45 MINUTES**

INGREDIENTS

3 tbsp olive oil
4 chicken quarters
450 g / 1 lb / 3 cups baby new potatoes
8 shallots, peeled
2 red peppers, cut into wedges
1 bulb of garlic, separated into cloves
salt and black pepper

GARNISH

2 tbsp flat leaf parsley, chopped

- Preheat the oven to 200°C (180°C fan) / 400F / gas 6.

- Heat the oil in a large roasting tin on the hob. Season the chicken with salt and pepper, then sear the skin in the oil.

- Stir in the potatoes, shallots, peppers and garlic, making sure everything is coated with the oil, then season with salt and pepper.

- Transfer the tin to the oven and roast for 15 minutes.

- Turn the heat down to 160°C (140°C fan) / 325F / gas 3 and roast for 1 hour 30 minutes stirring half way through. To check if the chicken is cooked, pierce the thickest part of a thigh with a skewer. If the juices run clear it's ready.

- Sprinkle the parsley over the dish and serve.

SERVES

4

Slow-roasted sirloin steak with fig sauce

PREPARATION TIME: **30 MINUTES** | COOKING TIME: **2 HOURS**

INGREDIENTS

4 thick sirloin steaks
2 tbsp olive oil
1 tbsp butter
3 small shallots, sliced
1 clove of garlic, crushed
1 tbsp concentrated tomato puree
125 ml / 4 ½ fl. oz / ½ cup Marsala
4 fresh figs, quartered
mashed potato to serve
salt and black pepper

- Preheat the oven to 130°C (110°C fan) / 250F / gas ½ and season the steaks liberally with salt and pepper.

- Heat the oil in a frying pan and sear the steaks on both sides. Transfer the steaks to a roasting tin then cover the tin with foil and roast for 2 hours, turning the steaks half way through.

- Remove the steaks from the oven, cover with a double layer of foil and leave to rest for 20 minutes.

- To make the sauce, put the steak frying pan back on the hob and add the butter. Fry the shallots for 5 minutes without colouring, then stir in the garlic and tomato puree. Pour in the Marsala and bubble for 2 minutes, then add the figs to the pan and warm through. Season to taste with salt and pepper.

- Serve the steaks with the sauce spooned over the top and some mashed potato on the side.

SERVES

4

Pot-roasted paupiettes of veal

PREPARATION TIME: 25 MINUTES | COOKING TIME: 1 HOUR

INGREDIENTS

4 good quality pork sausages, skinned
4 veal escallops
4 rashers smoked streaky bacon
2 tbsp olive oil
1 onion, sliced
2 carrots, sliced
1 bay leaf
150 ml / 5 ½ fl. oz / ⅔ cup dry white wine
150 ml / 5 ½ fl. oz / ⅔ cup veal stock
tagliatelle to serve
salt and black pepper

- Preheat the oven to 180°C (160°C fan) / 350F / gas 4.
- Put a quarter of the sausage meat on top of each escallop, then gather up the sides into a cushion shape. Wrap a rasher of bacon around each one, then tie securely with string.
- Heat the oil in a frying pan and sear the paupiettes on all sides.
- Transfer the paupiettes to a cast iron casserole dish and surround with the onion, carrots and bay leaf.
- Pour over the wine and stock then cover the pan and cook in the oven for 1 hour. Season to taste with salt and pepper then serve with tagliatelle.

SERVES

4

Beef in coconut milk

PREPARATION TIME: **15 MINUTES** | COOKING TIME: **6 HOURS**

INGREDIENTS

2 tbsp sunflower oil

450 g / 1 lb / 3 cups chuck steak, cut
    into large chunks

2 tbsp Thai yellow curry paste

8 large spring onions (scallions),
    peeled and halved

400 ml / 14 fl. oz / 1 ⅔ cups coconut
    milk

200 ml / 7 fl. oz / ¾ cup beef stock

1–2 tbsp fish sauce

2–3 tsp caster (superfine) sugar

coriander (cilantro leaves) to garnish

sweet potato mash to serve

- Heat the oil in a frying pan and sear the beef on all
  sides. Add the curry paste and onions to the pan and
  stir-fry for 2 minutes, then scrape the mixture into
  a slow cooker and stir in the coconut milk and stock.

- Cover and cook on medium for 6 hours, stirring
  every hour, then season to taste with fish sauce
  and sugar.

- Sprinkle with coriander leaves and serve with sweet
  potato mash.

Beef shin with carrots

PREPARATION TIME: 15 MINUTES | COOKING TIME: 6 HOURS

INGREDIENTS

450 g / 1 lb / 3 cups beef shin, cut into
   large chunks
2 tbsp plain (all purpose) flour
2 tbsp olive oil
1 onion, finely chopped
3 carrots, sliced
3 cloves of garlic, chopped
a few parsley stalks
700 ml / 1 pint 3 ½ fl. oz / 2 ¾ cups
   beef stock
salt and black pepper

GARNISH

2 tbsp curly parsley leaves, chopped

- Season the beef with salt and pepper and dust the pieces with flour to coat. Heat the oil in a large frying pan and sear the beef in batches on all sides. Transfer the beef to a slow cooker, then add the onion and carrots to the frying pan and cook without colouring for 5 minutes.

- Add the garlic and parsley stalks and cook for 1 more minute.

- Tip everything into a slow cooker and pour over the stock. Cover and cook on low for 6 hours, stirring every 2 hours. Season to taste with salt and pepper before serving, sprinkled with parsley.

SERVES

4

Slow-roasted hanger steak with salsa

PREPARATION TIME: **30 MINUTES** | COOKING TIME: **2 HOURS**

INGREDIENTS

4 hanger steaks
2 tbsp olive oil
1 small onion, finely chopped
2 large tomatoes, deseeded and finely
    chopped
2 large mild green chillies (chilies),
    deseeded and finely chopped
1 lime, juiced
mixed vegetable mash to serve
salt and black pepper

- Preheat the oven to 130°C (110°C fan) / 250F / gas ½ and season the steaks liberally with salt and pepper.

- Heat the oil in a frying pan and sear the steaks on both sides. Transfer the steaks to a roasting tin then cover the tin with foil and roast for 2 hours, turning the steaks half way through.

- Remove the steaks from the oven, cover with a double layer of foil and leave to rest for 20 minutes.

- To make the salsa, combine the onion, tomatoes and chilli in a bowl with the lime juice and season to taste with salt and pepper.

- Slice the steaks across the grain and spoon over the salsa. Serve with mixed vegetable mash.

SERVES

4

Pot-roasted paupiettes of pork with carrots

PREPARATION TIME: 25 MINUTES | COOKING TIME: 1 HOUR

INGREDIENTS

4 good quality pork sausages, skinned
4 pork escallops
2 tbsp olive oil
1 onion, sliced
2 carrots, sliced
2 bay leaves
a few sprigs of thyme
200 g / 7 oz / ¾ cup canned tomatoes, chopped
150 ml / 5 ½ fl. oz / ⅔ cup dry white wine
salt and black pepper

- Preheat the oven to 180°C (160°C fan) / 350F / gas 4.

- Put a quarter of the sausage meat on top of each escallop, then gather up the sides into a cushion shape and tie securely with string.

- Heat the oil in a frying pan and sear the paupiettes on all sides.

- Transfer the paupiettes to a cast iron casserole dish and surround with the onion, carrots, bay leaves and thyme. Stir the tomatoes into the wine, then pour it over the top.

- Cover the pan and cook in the oven for 1 hour. Season the vegetables to taste with salt and pepper just before serving.

SERVES

4

Pork and aubergine Colombo

PREPARATION TIME: 1 HOUR | COOKING TIME: 6 HOURS

INGREDIENTS

800 g / 1 lb 12 oz / 5 ⅓ cups pork
    shoulder, cubed
2 potatoes, peeled and cubed
1 aubergine (eggplant), cut into
    chunks
6 spring onions (scallions), chopped
2 cloves of garlic, finely chopped
2.5 cm (1 in) piece ginger, finely
    chopped
1 bay leaf
a few sprigs of thyme
2 tbsp Colombo seasoning or mild
    curry powder
400 ml / 14 fl. oz / 1 ⅔ cups chicken
    stock
200 ml / 7 fl. oz / ¾ cup light coconut
    milk
1 lime, juiced
salt and black pepper

- Mix the pork, potato, aubergine, spring onions, garlic, ginger, bay leaf and thyme together in a slow cooker. Sprinkle over the Colombo seasoning and leave to marinate for 1 hour.

- Pour in the stock and coconut milk then cover and cook on medium for 6 hours, stirring occasionally.

- Stir in the lime juice and season to taste with salt and pepper before serving.

SERVES

6

Braised oxtail with chorizo and turnip

PREPARATION TIME: **15 MINUTES** | COOKING TIME: **3 HOURS**

INGREDIENTS

6 thick slices oxtail, on the bone
4 tbsp olive oil
3 carrots, peeled and cut into chunks
3 large turnips, peeled and cut into
    chunks
2 bay leaves
a few sprigs of thyme
a few parsley stalks
½ chorizo ring, sliced
1 litre / 1 pint 15 fl. oz / 4 cups good
    quality beef stock

- Preheat the oven to 140°C (120°C fan) / 275F / gas 1.

- Heat half of the oil in a large cast iron casserole dish
  and sear the oxtail on both sides until well browned.

- Remove it from the dish, add the rest of the oil and fry
  the carrots and turnips for 5 minutes.

- Tie the bay leaves, thyme and parsley stalks into a
  bouquet garni with string and add it to the pot with
  the oxtail, chorizo and stock and bring to a simmer.

- Cover the casserole with a lid, transfer it to the oven
  and cook for 3 hours.

- Season to taste before serving.

SERVES

4

Chicken leg curry

PREPARATION TIME: 25 MINUTES | COOKING TIME: 6 HOURS

INGREDIENTS

2 tbsp sunflower oil

1 onion, chopped

1 red pepper, chopped

2 cloves of garlic, finely chopped

2.5 cm (1 in) piece ginger, finely
chopped

2 tbsp curry powder

400 ml / 14 fl. oz / 1 ⅔ cups chicken stock

400 ml / 14 fl. oz / 1 ⅔ cups tomato
passata

1 tbsp tamarind paste

8 chicken legs

rice salad to serve

sea salt

GARNISH

2 tbsp coriander (cilantro) leaves,
shredded

- Heat the oil in a frying pan and gently fry the onion, pepper, garlic and ginger for 15 minutes or until golden and sticky. Sprinkle in the curry powder and stir well, then transfer the mixture to a liquidiser. Add the stock, passata and tamarind paste and blend until smooth.

- Scrape the sauce into a slow cooker and add the chicken legs. Cover and cook on medium for 6 hours or until the chicken is very tender.

- Add salt to taste, then sprinkle with coriander and serve with a rice salad.

SERVES

4

Thai green meatball curry

PREPARATION TIME: **50 MINUTES** | COOKING TIME: **2 HOURS**

INGREDIENTS

400 ml / 14 fl. oz / 1 ⅔ cups chicken stock
400 ml / 14 fl. oz / 1 ⅔ cups coconut milk
2 kaffir lime leaves
3 tbsp green Thai curry paste
250 g / 9 oz/ 1 ⅔ cups raw prawns,
  finely chopped
250 g / 9 oz / 1 ⅔ cups pork sausage meat
1 tbsp sunflower oil
1–2 tbsp fish sauce
2–3 tsp caster (superfine) sugar
4 egg-sized aubergines (eggplants),
  quartered
4 spring onions (scallions), sliced
steamed rice to serve

GARNISH

coriander (cilantro) leaves

- Put the stock, coconut milk, lime leaves and 2 tbsp of the curry paste in a slow cooker, then cover and set it to medium.

- Mix the prawns and sausagemeat with the rest of the curry paste and ½ tsp of salt. Shape the mixture into walnut-sized meatballs and chill in the fridge to firm up for 30 minutes.

- Heat the oil in a large frying pan and sear the meatballs all over.

- Try the sauce in the slow cooker and add fish sauce and caster sugar to taste. Add the meatballs and aubergines, then cover and cook for 2 hours.

- Taste the curry again and adjust the seasoning if necessary, then stir in the spring onions and garnish with coriander before serving with steamed rice.

SERVES

4

Poached topside with vegetables

PREPARATION TIME: **10 MINUTES** | COOKING TIME: **8 HOURS**

INGREDIENTS

900 g / 2 lb beef topside
3 leeks, cut into short lengths
8 shallots, peeled
3 carrots, cut into chunks
150 g / 5 ½ oz / 1 cup runner beans, cut
   into short lengths
a few sprigs of thyme
salt and black pepper

- Put all of the ingredients in a slow cooker and pour over enough water to cover by 2.5 cm (1 in).

- Cover and cook on low for 8 hours. Season to taste then slice the beef and serve with the vegetables and cooking liquor.

SERVES

4

Chicken with chanterelles

PREPARATION TIME: 15 MINUTES | COOKING TIME: 3 HOURS 30 MINUTES

INGREDIENTS

2 tbsp butter
4 chicken breasts, halved
2 cloves of garlic, finely chopped
1 tbsp apricot brandy
300 ml / 10 ½ fl. oz / 1 ¼ cups chicken stock
600 ml / 1 pint / 2 ½ cups double (heavy) cream
225 g / 8 oz / 3 cups fresh chanterelles
salt and black pepper

- Heat the butter in a large frying pan and sear the chicken breasts on both sides. Transfer the chicken to a slow cooker and stir in the rest of the ingredients, except for the chanterelles.

- Cover and cook on low for 3 hours.

- Taste the sauce for seasoning and adjust with salt and black pepper. Stir in the chanterelles, then cover and cook for a further 30 minutes. Serve sprinkled with extra black pepper.

SERVES

4

Chicken blanquette

PREPARATION TIME: 15 MINUTES | COOKING TIME: 3 HOURS

INGREDIENTS

2 tbsp butter
4 chicken breasts
2 shallots, finely chopped
225 g / 8 oz / 3 cups button mushrooms
2 cloves of garlic, finely chopped
300 ml / 10 ½ fl. oz / 1 ¼ cups chicken
    stock
2 tbsp Pernod
600 ml / 1 pint / 2 ½ cups double
    (heavy) cream
salt and black pepper

GARNISH

1 tbsp French tarragon leaves

- Heat the butter in a large frying pan and sear the chicken breasts on both sides. Transfer the chicken to a slow cooker. Fry the shallots, mushrooms and garlic for 5 minutes without colouring, then scrape the mixture into the slow cooker.

- Pour over the stock, Pernod and cream, then cover and cook on low for 3 hours.

- Taste the sauce for seasoning and adjust with salt and black pepper. Serve garnished with tarragon.

SERVES

4

Chicken with figs and broad beans

PREPARATION TIME: 15 MINUTES | COOKING TIME: 2 HOURS 45 MINUTES

INGREDIENTS

4 tbsp olive oil

4 skinless chicken breasts, cut into chunks

1 onion, sliced

1 tbsp rosemary leaves

150 g / 5 ½ oz / 1 cup freshly shelled broad / fava beans

100 ml / 3 ½ fl. oz / ½ cup dry white wine

400 ml / 7 fl. oz / 1 ⅔ cups tomato passata

4 fresh figs, quartered

GARNISH

a few sprigs of coriander (cilantro)

- Heat the oil in a frying pan and sear the chicken pieces on all sides.

- Transfer to a slow cooker and stir in the rest of the ingredients, except for the figs and coriander.

- Cover and cook on high for 2 hours. Stir in the figs, then cover and cook for a further 45 minutes. Season to taste and serve garnished with coriander.

SERVES

4

Chicken curry

PREPARATION TIME: **15 MINUTES** | COOKING TIME: **3 HOURS**

INGREDIENTS

2 tbsp sunflower oil
1 onion, thinly sliced
2 cloves of garlic, finely chopped
2.5 cm (1 in) piece ginger, finely
    chopped
1 red pepper, chopped
2 tbsp curry powder
400 ml / 14 fl. oz / 1 ⅔ cups chicken
    stock
200 ml / 7 fl. oz / ¾ cup coconut milk
225 g / 8 oz / 1 cup chicken breast,
    sliced
1 lime, juiced
steamed rice to serve

GARNISH

a few sprigs of coriander (cilantro)

- Heat the oil in a saucepan and fry the onion, garlic, ginger and pepper for 5 minutes. Sprinkle in the curry powder and fry for 1 more minute, then pour in the stock and coconut milk.

- Bring the liquid to the boil, then stir in the chicken and transfer everything to a slow cooker.

- Cover and cook on medium for 3 hours. Try the sauce and add salt and lime juice to taste.

- Garnish the curry with coriander leaves and serve with steamed rice.

SERVES

4

Slow-roasted fillet steaks with shallots and garlic

PREPARATION TIME: **15 MINUTES** | COOKING TIME: **2 HOURS 30 MINUTES**

INGREDIENTS

4 x 5 cm (2 in) thick fillet steaks
2 tbsp olive oil
12 small shallots
12 cloves of garlic
salt and black pepper

- Preheat the oven to 130°C (110°C fan) / 250F / gas ½ and season the steaks liberally with salt and pepper.

- Heat the oil in a frying pan and sear the steaks on both sides. Transfer the steaks to a roasting tin and add the shallots and garlic. Cover the tin with foil and roast for 2 hours, turning the steaks half way through.

- Remove the steaks from the oven, leaving the tin with shallots and garlic inside, cover with a double layer of foil and leave to rest for 30 minutes.

- While the steaks are resting, increase the oven temperature to 180°C (160°C fan) / 350F / gas 4 to caramelise the shallots and garlic.

- Slice the steaks in half and serve with the shallots and garlic.

SERVES

6

Chicken legs with chickpeas and chorizo

PREPARATION TIME: **25 MINUTES** | COOKING TIME: **2 HOURS**

INGREDIENTS

400 g / 14 oz / 2 ⅔ cups dried
    chickpeas (garbanzo beans), soaked
    overnight
2 tbsp olive oil
6 chicken legs
1 red onion, sliced
1 carrot, peeled and chopped
1 celery stick, chopped
4 cloves of garlic, chopped
150 g / 5 ½ oz chorizo ring, sliced
2 tomatoes, cut into wedges
200 ml / 7 fl. oz / ¾ cup white wine

GARNISH

a few sprigs of coriander (cilantro)

- Preheat the oven to 160°C (140°C fan) / 325F / gas 3.

- Drain the chickpeas from their soaking water and put them in a large saucepan of cold water. Bring to the boil and cook for 10 minutes, then drain well.

- Heat the oil in a frying pan and sear the chicken legs on all sides. Remove the chicken from the pan then fry the onion, carrot, celery and garlic for 5 minutes without colouring.

- Tip the onion mixture into a baking dish and stir in the chorizo, tomatoes, wine and chickpeas.

- Arrange the chicken legs on top then cover with foil and bake for 1 hour 30 minutes.

- Remove the foil and bake for a further 30 minutes or until the chicken is browned and the chickpeas are tender. Serve garnished with coriander leaves.

SERVES

4

Paupiettes of veal with tomato sauce

PREPARATION TIME: 25 MINUTES | COOKING TIME: 1 HOUR

INGREDIENTS

4 good quality pork sausages, skinned
4 veal escallops
2 tbsp olive oil
1 onion, finely chopped
1 celery stick, finely chopped
4 cloves of garlic, finely chopped
1 bay leaf
150 ml / 5 ½ fl. oz / ⅔ cup dry white
    wine
150 ml / 5 ½ fl. oz / ⅔ cup veal stock
400 g / 14 oz / 1 ¾ cups canned
    tomatoes, chopped
salt and black pepper

- Preheat the oven to 180°C (160°C fan) / 350F / gas 4.

- Put a quarter of the sausage meat on top of each escallop, then gather up the sides into a cushion shape and tie securely with string.

- Heat the oil in a frying pan and sear the paupiettes on all sides.

- Transfer the paupiettes to a cast iron casserole dish, then add the carrots, celery and garlic to the frying pan and cook without colouring for 5 minutes.

- Scrape the vegetables into the casserole dish and stir in the rest of the ingredients, then cover the pan and cook in the oven for 1 hour. Season to taste with salt and pepper before serving.

SERVES

6-8

Slow-roasted brisket with tomatoes

PREPARATION TIME: 25 MINUTES | COOKING TIME: 5 HOURS 30 MINUTES

INGREDIENTS

2 tbsp butter
1 onion, finely chopped
2 cloves of garlic, crushed
75 g / 2 ½ oz / 1 cup fresh breadcrumbs
2 tbsp thyme leaves
2.5 kg / 5 ½ lb beef brisket
2 tbsp olive oil
6–8 small tomato vines
salt and black pepper

- Heat the butter in a frying pan and fry the onion and garlic with a big pinch of salt for 5 minutes or until softened, but not coloured. Take the pan off the heat and stir in the breadcrumbs and thyme. Leave to cool.

- Preheat the oven to 200°C (180°C fan) / 400F / gas 6. Unroll the beef brisket, then lay the stuffing in a line down the middle. Roll it back up and tie securely along the length with butchers' string.

- Rub the brisket all over with oil and season with salt and pepper, then transfer it to a shallow roasting tin and roast for 30 minutes.

- Reduce the oven to 140°C (120°C fan) / 275F / gas 1 and cover the brisket loosely with foil. Roast for 3 hours, basting every hour.

- Remove the foil and arrange the tomato vines around the outside of the beef, then return to the oven for 2 hours or until the beef is tender and the tomatoes are starting to collapse.

- Cover the roasting tin and leave to rest somewhere warm for 30 minutes before carving into thick slices.

SERVES

4

Slow-cooked beef with mushrooms

PREPARATION TIME: 20 MINUTES | COOKING TIME: 6 HOURS

INGREDIENTS

450 g / 1 lb / 3 cups chuck steak, cut
    into large chunks
2 tbsp plain (all purpose) flour
2 tbsp olive oil
2 onions, cut into thin wedges
3 cloves of garlic, chopped
2 bay leaves
a few sprigs thyme
700 ml / 1 pint 3 ½ fl. oz / 2 ¾ cups dry
    white wine
225 g / 8 oz / 3 cups button
    mushrooms, sliced
flat leaf parsley to garnish

- Season the beef with salt and pepper and dust the pieces with flour to coat. Heat the oil in a large frying pan and sear the beef in batches on all sides. Transfer the beef to a slow cooker, then add the onions and garlic to the frying pan and cook without colouring for 5 minutes.

- Stir in the herbs then pour in the wine and bring to the boil. Tip everything into the slow cooker, then cover and cook on low for 5 hours.

- Stir in the mushrooms, then cover and cook for another hour.

- Season to taste with salt and pepper before serving, garnished with parsley.

SERVES

4

Poached beef with ginger

PREPARATION TIME: 15 MINUTES | COOKING TIME: 6 HOURS

INGREDIENTS

2 tbsp sunflower oil

450 g / 1 lb / 3 cups chuck steak, cut
into large chunks

30 g / 1 oz piece of fresh root ginger,
sliced

2 lemongrass stalks, bruised

4 spring onions (scallions), bruised

1 bulb of garlic, halved horizontally

a few coriander (cilantro) stalks

75 ml / 2 ½ fl. oz / ⅓ cup shaoxing rice
wine

75 ml / 2 ½ fl. oz / ⅓ cup light soy
sauce

GARNISH

a few sprigs of coriander (cilantro)

- Heat the oil in a frying pan and sear the beef on all
sides. Transfer the beef to a slow cooker and add the
rest of the ingredients.

- Add enough cold water to cover the beef, then cover
the slow cooker and cook on low for 6 hours.

- Drain the beef and serve garnished with coriander.
The cooking liquor can be strained and served as a
broth or used for stock in another recipe.

SERVES

6

Meatballs in tomato sauce

PREPARATION TIME: **35 MINUTES** | COOKING TIME: **3 HOURS**

INGREDIENTS

4 tbsp olive oil
1 onion, finely chopped
1 clove of garlic, crushed
1 red chilli (chili), deseeded and finely
    chopped
250 g / 9 oz minced veal
250 g / 9 oz sausagemeat
50 g fresh white breadcrumbs
1 tsp dried oregano
1 egg yolk
1 sprig of rosemary
600 ml / 1 pint / 2 ½ cups tomato
    passata
salt and black pepper

- Heat half of the oil in a large sauté pan and fry the onion for 5 minutes or until softened.

- Add the garlic and chilli and cook for 2 more minutes, stirring constantly, then scrape the mixture into a mixing bowl and leave to cool.

- Add the mince, sausagemeat, breadcrumbs, oregano and egg yolk and mix well, then shape into golf ball-sized meatballs.

- Heat the rest of the oil in the sauté pan and sear the meatballs on all sides, then season with salt and pepper.

- Arrange the meatballs in a single layer in a slow cooker and tuck the rosemary sprig into the middle. Pour over the passata, then cover and cook on medium for 3 hours. Season to taste before serving.

SERVES

4

Slow-cooked beef in red wine with carrots

PREPARATION TIME: 20 MINUTES | COOKING TIME: 6 HOURS

INGREDIENTS

450 g / 1 lb / 3 cups chuck steak, cut
   into large chunks
2 tbsp plain (all purpose) flour
2 tbsp olive oil
1 onion, chopped
2 carrots, chopped
3 cloves of garlic, chopped
2 tbsp concentrated tomato puree
2 bay leaves
a few sprigs thyme
1 orange, zest pared into thick strips
700 ml / 1 pint 3 ½ fl. oz / 2 ¾ cups
   red wine
salt and black pepper

- Season the beef with salt and pepper and dust the pieces with flour to coat. Heat the oil in a large frying pan and sear the beef in batches on all sides. Transfer the beef to a slow cooker, then put the onion and carrots to the frying pan and cook without colouring for 5 minutes.

- Add the garlic, tomato puree and herbs to the pan and cook for 1 more minute. Pour in the wine and bring to the boil, then tip everything into the slow cooker.

- Put the lid on the slow cooker and cook on low for 6 hours, stirring every 2 hours. Season to taste with salt and pepper before serving.

Slow-cooked turkey blanquette

PREPARATION TIME: **15 MINUTES** | COOKING TIME: **4 HOURS**

INGREDIENTS

2 tbsp butter
800 g / 1 lb 12 oz turkey breast, cubed
2 tbsp plain (all purpose) flour
1 leek, finely chopped
2 carrots, julienned
2 courgettes (zucchini), julienned
600 ml / 1 pint / 2 ½ cups light veal or
    chicken stock
300 ml / 10 ½ fl. oz / 1 ¼ cups double
    (heavy) cream
2 tbsp curly parsley, chopped
salt and black pepper

- Heat the butter in a frying pan. Dust the turkey pieces with flour and season with salt and pepper, then sear them all over.

- Transfer the turkey to a slow cooker and mix with the rest of the ingredients, except for the parsley.

- Cook on low for 4 hours, then taste the sauce for seasoning and adjust with salt and black pepper. Stir in the parsley and serve.

SERVES

4

Chicken with mozzarella and herbs

PREPARATION TIME: **30 MINUTES** | COOKING TIME: **2 HOURS**

INGREDIENTS

4 skinless chicken breasts
2 mozzarella balls, quartered
4 tbsp olive oil
½ tbsp fresh thyme leaves
1 tbsp flat leaf parsley, finely chopped
1 tbsp chives, finely chopped
grilled tomatoes to serve

- Half fill a slow cooker with water and put it on low to preheat for 1 hour.

- Lay each chicken breast between two sheets of clingfilm and bash them flat with a rolling pin. Discard the top layer of clingfilm, then arrange two pieces of mozzarella down the centre of each chicken breast.

- Roll up the chicken breasts and wrap tightly in a double layer of clingfilm, twisting the ends to seal.

- Put the oil and herbs in a small zip-lock sandwich bag and exclude as much air as possible before sealing it.

- Lower the chicken and oil bag into the slow cooker, weighing them down with a trivet if they try to float. Cover and poach for 2 hours.

- Carefully unwrap the chicken and cut into thick slices. Serve with grilled tomatoes and the herb oil drizzled over.

SERVES

4

Lamb chops with tomato sauce

PREPARATION TIME: 15 MINUTES | COOKING TIME: 2 HOURS

INGREDIENTS

4 tbsp olive oil

8 lamb chops

4 rashers back bacon

2 bulbs of fennel, thickly sliced

1 onion, sliced

1 tbsp rosemary leaves

150 g / 5 ½ oz / 2 cups button
    mushrooms, sliced

100 ml / 3 ½ fl. oz / ½ cup dry white
    wine

400 ml / 7 fl. oz / 1 ⅔ cups tomato
    passata

GARNISH

a few sprigs of basil

- Heat the oil in a frying pan and sear the lamb chops on both sides, followed by the bacon. Transfer to a slow cooker and add the rest of the ingredients.

- Cover and cook on high for 2 hours, then garnish with basil and serve.

FISH

SERVES

4

Poached salmon with vegetable julienne

PREPARATION TIME: 35 MINUTES | COOKING TIME: 45 MINUTES

INGREDIENTS

1 tbsp butter
2 shallots, finely chopped
150 ml / 5 ½ fl. oz / ⅔ cup dry white
   wine
150 ml / 5 ½ fl. oz / ⅔ cup fish stock
2 leeks, julienned
2 carrots, julienned
1 fennel bulb, julienned
4 portions of salmon fillet
100 ml / 3 ½ fl. oz / ½ cup double
   (heavy) cream
2 tbsp French tarragon leaves,
   chopped
salt and black pepper

- Preheat the oven to 150°C (130°C fan) / 300F / gas 2.

- Heat the butter in a wide ovenproof saucepan and fry the shallots gently for 5 minutes without colouring. Pour in the white wine and boil off the alcohol for 2 minutes, then add the stock.

- Bring the pan to a gentle simmer, then add the vegetables and simmer for 3 minutes. Lay the salmon on top in a single layer. Cover the pan and transfer it to the oven then cook for 45 minutes.

- Transfer the salmon to 4 warm bowls and bring the sauce back to the boil on the hob. Stir in the cream and season to taste with salt and pepper. Take the pan off the heat and stir in the tarragon, then spoon the sauce and vegetables over the salmon.

SERVES

4

Pot-roasted cod with fennel stems

PREPARATION TIME: 25 MINUTES | COOKING TIME: 45 MINUTES

INGREDIENTS

12 x 13 cm (5 in) wild fennel stems
4 portions of cod fillet
150 ml / 5 ½ fl. oz / ⅔ cup dry white wine
150 ml / 5 ½ fl. oz / ⅔ cup fish stock
½ lemon, juiced
75 g / 2 ½ oz / ⅓ cup butter, cubed
1 tbsp fennel fronds, finely chopped
seasonal vegetables to serve
salt and black pepper

- Preheat the oven to 150°C (130°C fan) / 300F / gas 2.

- Lay the fennel stems in a single layer in an oven-proof casserole dish to form a trivet and space out the cod portions on top.

- Bring the wine and stock to the boil in a small saucepan, then pour it over the cod. Cover the casserole dish, transfer it to the oven and cook for 45 minutes.

- Transfer the cod and fennel stems to four warm plates, then stir the lemon juice into the cooking liquid. Whisk in the butter a few cubes at a time until smoothly homogenised, then stir in the fennel fronds and season to taste with salt and pepper.

- Spoon the sauce over the cod and serve with seasonal vegetables.

SERVES

4

Confit peppers with sea bass

PREPARATION TIME: 20 MINUTES | COOKING TIME: 4 HOURS

INGREDIENTS

8 red peppers
300 ml / 10 ½ fl. oz olive oil
2 sea bass fillets
50 g / 1 ¾ oz / ⅓ cup mixed olives
a handful of basil leaves
salt and black pepper

- Remove the stalks from the peppers, then cut them into quarters and discard the seeds. Lay them skin side down in a slow cooker and pour over the olive oil. Cover and cook on medium for 4 hours, then leave to cool completely in the oil.

- Drain off the oil, reserving it for future confiting or salad dressings, then peel off and discard the pepper skins.

- Season the sea bass with salt and pepper, then cook under the grill for 3 minutes on each side or until just opaque in the centre.

- Serve the sea bass with the confit peppers and the olives and basil leaves scattered around.

SERVES

4

Pike perch with sorrel sauce

PREPARATION TIME: 35 MINUTES | COOKING TIME: 45 MINUTES

INGREDIENTS

1 large carrot, julienned
1 fennel bulb, julienned
4 tbsp sorrel leaves, shredded
4 pike perch fillets, skinned and
  boned
1 tbsp butter
2 shallots, finely chopped
150 ml / 5 ½ fl. oz / ⅔ cup dry white
  wine
150 ml / 5 ½ fl. oz / ⅔ cup fish stock
100 ml / 3 ½ fl. oz / ½ cup double
  (heavy) cream
wild rice to serve
salt and black pepper

- Preheat the oven to 150°C (130°C fan) / 300F / gas 2.
  Bring a pan of salted water to the boil then add the
  carrots and fennel and simmer for 10 minutes or until
  tender. Drain well.

- Toss the vegetables with half of the sorrel, then divide
  the mixture between the perch fillets, roll them up
  and secure with wooden skewers.

- Heat the butter in a wide ovenproof saucepan and fry
  the shallots gently for 5 minutes without colouring.
  Pour in the white wine and boil off the alcohol for
  2 minutes, then add the stock.

- Bring the pan to a gentle simmer, then add the pike
  perch in a single layer. Cover the pan and transfer it to
  the oven then cook for 45 minutes.

- Transfer the pike perch to a warm plate and bring the
  sauce back to the boil on the hob. Stir in the cream
  and season to taste with salt and pepper. Take the pan
  off the heat and stir in the sorrel.

- Serve the paupiettes with wild rice and the sauce
  spooned over the top.

SERVES

4

Monkfish with mango and coconut milk

PREPARATION TIME: 25 MINUTES | COOKING TIME: 45 MINUTES

INGREDIENTS

8 large monkfish cutlets

8 rashers pancetta

1 tbsp butter

2 shallots, finely chopped

2.5 cm (1 in) piece fresh root ginger,
   finely chopped

3 cloves of garlic, finely chopped

400 ml / 14 fl. oz / 1 ⅔ cups coconut
   milk

150 ml / 5 ½ fl. oz / ⅔ cup fish stock

2 tsp mild curry powder

2 mangos, peeled, stoned and diced

GARNISH

coriander (cilantro leaves)

- Preheat the oven to 150°C (130°C fan) / 300F / gas 2. Wrap the monkfish in pancetta and tie securely with string.

- Heat the butter in a wide ovenproof saucepan and fry the shallots, ginger and garlic gently for 5 minutes without colouring. Stir in the coconut milk, stock and curry powder and bring to a simmer, then stir in the mango.

- Position the monkfish on top then cover the pan and cook it in the oven for 45 minutes.

- Season the sauce to taste then serve garnished with coriander.

SERVES

4

Sea bass paupiettes

PREPARATION TIME: 25 MINUTES | COOKING TIME: 45 MINUTES

INGREDIENTS

300 g / 10 ½ oz / 1 cup chargrilled
    artichokes in oil, drained
1 tbsp French tarragon leaves
8 sea bass fillets, skinned and boned
1 tbsp butter
2 shallots, finely chopped
150 ml / 5 ½ fl. oz / ⅔ cup dry white
    wine
150 ml / 5 ½ fl. oz / ⅔ cup fish stock
a pinch of saffron
mashed potato to serve
salt and black pepper

- Preheat the oven to 150°C (130°C fan) / 300F / gas 2.

- Roughly chop the artichokes and mix them with the tarragon. Lay out the sea bass fillets and divide the artichoke mixture between them. Roll up the fillets and tie them securely with string.

- Heat the butter in a wide ovenproof saucepan and fry the shallots gently for 5 minutes without colouring. Pour in the white wine and boil off the alcohol for 2 minutes, then add the stock and saffron.

- Bring the pan to a gentle simmer, then add the paupiettes in a single layer. Cover the pan and transfer it to the oven then cook for 45 minutes.

- Season the sauce to taste then serve two paupiettes per person with mashed potato and the sauce spooned over the top.

STEWS & TAGINES

SERVES

4

Salmon and vegetable stew

PREPARATION TIME: **15 MINUTES** | COOKING TIME: **2 HOURS 5 MINUTES**

INGREDIENTS

2 tbsp olive oil
1 onion, finely chopped
2 cloves of garlic, crushed
2 large potatoes, peeled and cubed
1 green romano pepper, sliced
1 bay leaf
600 ml / 1 pint / 2 ½ cups fish stock
400 g / 14 oz / 2 cups canned tomatoes, chopped
4 thick salmon steaks

- Heat the oil in a wide saucepan and fry the onion for 5 minutes or until softened. Add the garlic and cook for 2 more minutes then stir in the potatoes, pepper and bay leaf.

- Pour in the stock and tomatoes and bring to the boil. Season to taste with salt and pepper.

- Arrange the salmon steaks in a snug single layer in a slow cooker and pour over the vegetables and stock.

- Cover the slow cooker and cook on low for 2 hours.

SERVES

4

Seafood and vegetable stew

PREPARATION TIME: **15 MINUTES** | COOKING TIME: **1 HOUR**

INGREDIENTS

3 tbsp olive oil
1 onion, chopped
2 carrots, peeled and sliced
2 cloves of garlic, crushed
175 ml / 6 fl. oz / ⅔ cup dry white wine
a pinch of saffron
500 ml / 17 ½ fl. oz / 2 cups fish stock
3 tbsp concentrated tomato puree
600 ml / 1 pint / 2 ½ cups live mussels,
   scrubbed
12 king prawns, heads removed
1 large monkfish tail, boned and cut
   into chunks
150 g / 5 ½ oz / 1 cup peas

- Heat the oil in a sauté pan and fry the onion and carrots for 5 minutes to soften without colouring. Add the garlic and cook for 1 more minute, then pour in the wine and reduce by half.

- Stir in the saffron, stock and tomato puree and bring to a simmer, then transfer the contents of the pan to a slow cooker and stir in the mussels, prawns, monkfish and peas.

- Cover the slow cooker and cook on medium for 1 hour or until all of the mussels have opened.

SERVES

4

Boeuf bourguignon

PREPARATION TIME: **20 MINUTES** | COOKING TIME: **6 HOURS**

INGREDIENTS

450 g / 1 lb / 3 cups chuck steak, cut
  into large chunks
2 tbsp plain (all purpose) flour
2 tbsp olive oil
150 g / 5 ½ oz / 1 cup bacon lardons
12 small shallots, peeled
1 large carrot, chopped
1 celery stick, chopped
3 cloves of garlic, chopped
2 tbsp concentrated tomato puree
2 bay leaves
a few sprigs thyme
700 ml / 1 pint 3 ½ fl. oz / 2 ¾ cups
  red wine
150 g / 5 ½ oz / 2 cups baby button
  mushrooms
salt and black pepper

GARNISH

2 tbsp flat leaf parsley, chopped

- Season the beef with salt and pepper and dust the pieces with flour to coat. Heat the oil in a large frying pan and sear the beef in batches on all sides.

- Transfer the beef to a slow cooker, then add the lardons, shallots, carrots, celery and garlic to the frying pan and cook without colouring for 5 minutes.

- Stir in the tomato puree and herbs then pour in the wine and bring to the boil. Transfer the contents of the frying pan to a slow cooker.

- Cover the slow cooker and cook on low for 5 hours. Add the mushrooms and cook for 1 more hour.

- Season to taste with salt and pepper, then serve sprinkled with parsley.

125

SERVES

4

Pork and peach stew

PREPARATION TIME: **15 MINUTES** | COOKING TIME: **5 HOURS**

INGREDIENTS

2 tbsp butter

800 g / 1 lb 12 oz / 5 ⅓ cups pork
   shoulder, cubed

1 onion, quartered and sliced

2 medium potatoes, peeled and cubed

2 tbsp peach schnapps

600 ml / 1 pint / 2 ½ cups chicken
   stock

3 peaches, peeled, stoned and cubed

salt and black pepper

GARNISH

2 tbsp curly parsley leaves, chopped

- Heat the butter in a large frying pan and sear the pork on all sides. Transfer the pork to a slow cooker and stir in the rest of the ingredients, except for the peaches and parsley.

- Cover and cook on low for 4 hours.

- Stir in the peaches and cook for 1 hour. Taste the sauce for seasoning and adjust with salt and black pepper.

- Spoon into individual warmed casserole dishes and serve garnished with parsley.

SERVES

4

Chicken and preserved lemon tagine

PREPARATION TIME: 15 MINUTES | COOKING TIME: 2 HOURS

INGREDIENTS

2 tbsp olive oil
1 chicken, jointed
1 onion, diced
2 cloves of garlic, sliced
1 tsp ground coriander (cilantro)
1 tsp ground ginger
a pinch of saffron
2 small preserved lemons, quartered
100 g / 3 ½ oz / ⅔ cup kalamata olives
250 ml / 9 fl. oz / 1 cup chicken stock
sea salt

GARNISH

fennel fronds

- Preheat the oven to 160°C (140°C fan) / 325F / gas 3.

- Heat the oil in a large frying pan and season the chicken with salt. Sear the chicken pieces on all sides, then transfer to a tagine.

- Add the onion, garlic, spices, preserved lemon and olives to the tagine and mix well. Pour over the stock then put on the lid and transfer the tagine to the oven.

- Cook the tagine for 2 hours, then garnish with fennel and serve.

SERVES

6

Mixed pulse stew

PREPARATION TIME: **20 MINUTES** | COOKING TIME: **6 HOURS 30 MINUTES**

INGREDIENTS

150 g / 5 ½ oz / 1 cup dried broad
  beans (fava beans), soaked
  overnight
150 g / 5 ½ oz / 1 cup dried chickpeas
  (garbanzo beans), soaked overnight
100 g / 3 ½ oz / ½ cup green lentils
100 g / 3 ½ oz / ½ cup pearl barley
2 medium potatoes, peeled and diced
1 onion, finely chopped
4 cloves of garlic, chopped
1 bay leaf
½ head of broccoli, diced
salt and black pepper

- Drain the beans and chickpeas from their soaking water and put them in a large saucepan of cold water. Bring to the boil and cook for 10 minutes, then drain well.

- Mix the beans with the lentils, barley, potatoes, onion, garlic and bay leaf in a slow cooker. Pour over enough boiling water to cover everything by 5 cm (2 in), then cook on low for 6 hours or until the pulses are tender, but still holding their shape.

- Season to taste with salt and pepper, then stir in the broccoli and cook for a further 30 minutes.

SERVES

6

Shellfish chowder

PREPARATION TIME: 15 MINUTES | COOKING TIME: 1 HOUR 15 MINUTES

INGREDIENTS

2 shallots, finely chopped
2 cloves of garlic, crushed
175 ml / 6 fl. oz / ⅔ cup dry white wine
600 ml / 1 pint / 2 ½ cups live mussels,
   scrubbed
600 ml / 1 pint / 2 ½ cups live whelks,
   scrubbed
600 ml / 1 pint / 2 ½ cups live large
   clams, scrubbed
6 langoustines
12 scallops, sliced in half horizontally
500 ml / 17 ½ fl. oz / 2 cups fish stock
1 bay leaf
250 ml / 9 fl. oz / 1 cup double (heavy)
   cream

GARNISH

a few sprigs of chervil
mild curry powder for sprinkling

- Put all of the ingredients except for the cream, chervil and curry powder in a slow cooker and cook on medium for 1 hour.

- Stir in the cream and cook for a further 15 minutes or until the mussels and clams have opened.

- Ladle the chowder into warm bowls and garnish with the chervil and a sprinkle of curry powder.

SERVES

6

Vegetarian hot pot

PREPARATION TIME: 25 MINUTES | COOKING TIME: 3 HOURS 10 MINUTES

INGREDIENTS

2 tbsp olive oil

1 onion, sliced

1 red pepper, diced

2 cloves of garlic, crushed

450 g / 1 lb / 2 cups vegetarian mince

400 g / 14 oz / 1 ¾ cups canned
  tomatoes, chopped

200 ml / 7 fl. oz / ¾ cup vegetable
  stock

400 g / 14 oz / 1 ¾ cups canned haricot
  beans, drained

400 g / 14 oz / 2 cups maris piper
  potatoes, sliced

50 g / 1 ¾ oz / ¼ cup butter, cubed

- Preheat the oven to 160°C (140°C fan) / 325F / gas 3.

- Heat the oil in a large frying pan and fry the onion, pepper and garlic for 10 minutes, stirring occasionally. Add the mince and fry until it starts to brown then stir in the tomatoes, stock and beans.

- Scrape the mixture into a baking dish and arrange the potato slices in top. Cover the dish with foil and bake for 2 hours.

- Remove the foil and dot the surface of the hot pot with butter then bake for 1 more hour.

SERVES

4

Chicken, potato and pepper tagine

PREPARATION TIME: 20 MINUTES | COOKING TIME: 2 HOURS

INGREDIENTS

2 tbsp olive oil

4 chicken legs

1 onion, sliced

4 small potatoes, cut into wedges

1 red pepper, diced

3 cloves of garlic, finely chopped

2.5 cm (1 in) piece fresh root ginger, finely chopped

1 tsp ground cumin

1 tsp ground coriander (cilantro)

1 tsp ground ginger

a pinch of saffron

250 ml / 9 fl. oz / 1 cup chicken stock

- Preheat the oven to 160°C (140°C fan) / 325F / gas 3.

- Heat the oil in a large frying pan and season the chicken with salt. Sear the chicken legs on all sides, then transfer to a tagine.

- Mix with in the rest of the ingredients, then put on the lid and transfer the tagine to the oven.

- Cook the tagine for 2 hours, then leave to stand for 15 minutes before serving.

SERVES

6

Ham and bean stew

PREPARATION TIME: 25 MINUTES | COOKING TIME: 6 HOURS

INGREDIENTS

225 g / 8 oz piece boiling ham, diced
1 onion, finely chopped
1 celery stick, sliced
1 carrot, chopped
2 cloves of garlic, crushed
1 medium tomato, diced
300 g / 10 ½ oz / 2 cups haricot beans,
    soaked overnight
1.2 litres / 2 pint / 5 cups vegetable
    stock
1 bay leaf
salt and black pepper

- Stir all of the ingredients together in a slow cooker, then cover and cook on medium for 6 hours.

- Taste the soup for seasoning and adjust with salt and pepper, then ladle into warm bowls and serve.

SERVES

6

Chicken, potato and bean stew

PREPARATION TIME: 20 MINUTES | COOKING TIME: 6 HOURS

INGREDIENTS

150 g / 5 ½ oz / 1 cup dried haricot
  beans, soaked overnight
150 g / 5 ½ oz / 1 cup dried chickpeas
  (garbanzo beans), soaked overnight
450 g / 1 lb / 3 cups chicken breast,
  diced
2 medium potatoes, sliced
2 carrots, chopped
1 onion, finely chopped
4 cloves of garlic, chopped
400 ml / 14 fl. oz / 1 ⅔ cups chicken
  stock
400 ml / 14 fl. oz / 1 ⅔ cups tomato
  passata
100 g / 3 ½ oz / 4 cups spinach, washed
salt and black pepper

- Drain the beans and chickpeas from their soaking water and put them in a large saucepan of cold water. Bring to the boil and cook for 10 minutes, then drain well.

- Mix the beans with the rest of the ingredients, except for the spinach, in a slow cooker. Cover and cook on low for 6 hours or until the pulses are tender, but still holding their shape.

- Season to taste with salt and pepper, then stir in the spinach, cover the pan and leave to wilt for 5 minutes.

SERVES

6

Beef, chorizo and mushroom stew

PREPARATION TIME: 20 MINUTES | COOKING TIME: 6 HOURS

INGREDIENTS

450 g / 1 lb / 3 cups chuck steak, cut
   into large chunks
2 tbsp plain (all purpose) flour
2 tbsp olive oil
1 chorizo ring, sliced diagonally
3 cloves of garlic, chopped
2 bay leaves
700 ml / 1 pint 3 ½ fl. oz / 2 ¾ cups
   beef stock
225 g / 8 oz / 3 cups baby button
   mushrooms
salt and black pepper

GARNISH

rocket (arugula) leaves

- Season the beef with salt and pepper and dust the pieces with flour to coat. Heat the oil in a large frying pan and sear the beef in batches on all sides. Transfer the beef to a slow cooker, then sear the chorizo pieces on both sides and add them to the beef.

- Stir the garlic, bay leaves and stock into the slow cooker, then cover and cook on low for 5 hours.

- Stir in the mushrooms, then cover and cook for another hour.

- Season to taste with salt and pepper before serving. Garnish with rocket leaves.

SERVES

4

Chicken and vegetables with cashew nuts

PREPARATION TIME: 15 MINUTES | COOKING TIME: 3 HOURS

INGREDIENTS

2 tbsp sunflower oil
1 onion, thinly sliced
2 cloves of garlic, finely chopped
2.5 cm (1 in) piece ginger, finely
    chopped
1 red pepper, sliced
1 courgette (zucchini), julienned
2 runner beans, thinly sliced
2 tbsp curry powder
400 ml / 14 fl. oz / 1 ⅔ cups chicken
    stock
200 ml / 7 fl. oz / ¾ cup coconut milk
225 g / 8 oz / 1 cup chicken breast,
    cubed
1 lime, juiced
75 g / 2 ½ oz / ⅔ cup roasted cashew
    nuts, roughly chopped
steamed rice to serve
pinch of salt

GARNISH

coriander (cilantro leaves)

- Heat the oil in a saucepan and fry the onion, garlic, ginger, pepper, courgette and beans for 5 minutes. Sprinkle in the curry powder and fry for 1 more minute, then pour in the stock and coconut milk.

- Bring the liquid to the boil, then stir in the chicken and transfer everything to a slow cooker.

- Cover and cook on medium for 3 hours. Try the sauce and add salt and lime juice to taste.

- Stir in the cashew nuts, then garnish with coriander leaves and serve with steamed rice.

SERVES

4

Slow-cooked brisket pot au feu

PREPARATION TIME: 10 MINUTES | COOKING TIME: 8 HOURS

INGREDIENTS

450 g / 1 lb beef brisket
8 small turnips, scrubbed
4 salad onions, peeled
4 carrots, peeled
8 waxy potatoes, peeled
3 cloves of garlic, sliced
2 bay leaves

- Put all of the ingredients in a slow cooker and pour over enough water to cover by 2.5 cm (1 in).

- Cover and cook on low for 8 hours. Cut the beef into chunks or slices and serve with the vegetables and cooking liquor.

SERVES

4

Ham pot au feu

PREPARATION TIME: 10 MINUTES | COOKING TIME: 8 HOURS

INGREDIENTS

450 g / 1 lb piece of boiling ham
4 turnips, scrubbed and quartered
2 leeks, thickly sliced
2 small carrots, peeled and sliced
2 small purple carrots, peeled and
   sliced
2 bay leaves
½ savoy cabbage, cut into wedges

- Put all of the ingredients, except for the cabbage in a slow cooker and pour over enough water to cover by 2.5 cm (1 in).

- Cover and cook on low for 8 hours, adding the cabbage after 6 hours. Cut the ham into chunks or slices and serve with the vegetables and cooking liquor.

149

SERVES

Stewed peppers and tomatoes

PREPARATION TIME: 20 MINUTES | COOKING TIME: 3 HOURS 30 MINUTES

INGREDIENTS

3 tbsp olive oil
1 onion, sliced
2 red peppers, cut into chunks
2 yellow peppers, cut into chunks
2 green peppers, cut into chunks
2 cloves of garlic, sliced
4 medium tomatoes
4 tbsp dry sherry
250 ml / 9 fl. oz / 1 cup vegetable stock
salt and black pepper

- Put the oil in a slow cooker and heat on high. Stir in the onion and peppers and season with salt and pepper. Cover and cook for 1 hour 30 minutes, stirring every 15 minutes.

- Stir in the garlic, tomatoes and sherry, then pour over the vegetable stock.

- Cover and cook on low for 2 hours. Season to taste before serving.

SERVES

4

Hake and potato stew

PREPARATION TIME: **10 MINUTES** | COOKING TIME: **4 HOURS**

INGREDIENTS

3 medium potatoes, peeled and cubed
1 onion, finely chopped
1 fennel bulb, finely chopped
3 cloves of garlic, finely chopped
1 tsp smoked paprika
2 tbsp concentrated tomato puree
600 ml / 1 pint / 2 ½ cups fish stock
2 kg / 4 lbs 6 oz hake, cut into steaks
salt and black pepper

- Mix all of the ingredients together, except for the hake, in a slow cooker.

- Cover and cook on medium for 3 hours or until the potatoes are tender, but still holding their shape.

- Arrange the hake steaks on top, then cover the cooker and cook for a further 1 hour or until the fish is just opaque in the centre.

- Season to taste with salt and pepper, then ladle into warm bowls to serve.

SERVES

4

Beef, turnip and lardon stew

PREPARATION TIME: 20 MINUTES | COOKING TIME: 6 HOURS

INGREDIENTS

450 g / 1 lb / 3 cups stewing beef, cubed
2 tbsp plain (all purpose) flour
2 tbsp olive oil
100 g / 2 ⅓ oz / ½ cup lardons
6 small turnips, peeled and halved
125 ml / 4 ½ fl. oz / ½ cup red wine
1 onion, finely chopped
3 cloves of garlic, crushed
2 bay leaves
½ orange, zest pared into thin strips
500 ml / 17 ½ fl. oz / 2 cups good quality beef stock
salt and black pepper

- Season the beef with salt and pepper and dust the pieces with flour to coat. Heat the oil in a large frying pan and sear the beef in batches on all sides.

- Transfer the beef to a slow cooker, then fry the lardons and turnips in the frying pan until lightly coloured. Deglaze the pan with the wine, then tip everything into the slow cooker and stir in the rest of the ingredients. Season well with salt and pepper.

- Put the lid on the slow cooker and cook on low for 6 hours, stirring every 2 hours.

SERVES

4

Ox cheek and stout stew

PREPARATION TIME: 15 MINUTES | COOKING TIME: 6 HOURS

INGREDIENTS

4 portions of ox cheek
4 tbsp plain (all purpose) flour
2 tbsp butter
1 onion, finely chopped
3 cloves of garlic, chopped
1 tbsp Dijon mustard
2 bay leaves
1 tbsp Worcestershire sauce
700 ml / 1 pint 3 ½ fl. oz / 2 ¾ cups
   stout
225 g / 8 oz / 3 cups baby button
   mushrooms, halved
mashed potato to serve
salt and black pepper

- Season the ox cheek with salt and pepper and dust with flour to coat. Heat the butter in a large frying pan and sear the pieces on all sides.

- Transfer the ox cheek to a slow cooker, then add the onion and garlic to the frying pan and cook without colouring for 5 minutes.

- Stir in the mustard, bay leaves and Worcestershire sauce, then pour in the stout and bring to the boil.

- Scrape the contents of the pan into the slow cooker along with the ox cheek, then cover and cook on low for 4 hours, stirring half way through. Stir in the mushrooms and cook for another 2 hours or until the ox cheeks are very tender.

- Season the sauce to taste with salt and pepper and serve with mashed potato.

SERVES

6

Chilli con carne

PREPARATION TIME: 25 MINUTES | COOKING TIME: 5 HOURS

INGREDIENTS

2 tbsp olive oil

1 onion, finely chopped

1 red pepper, diced

1 red chilli (chili), finely chopped

2 cloves of garlic, crushed

½ tsp cayenne pepper, plus extra for
    sprinkling

450 g / 1 lb / 2 cups minced beef

400 g / 14 oz / 1 ¾ cups canned
    tomatoes, chopped

200 ml / 7 fl. oz / ¾ cup beef stock

400 g / 14 oz / 1 ¾ cups canned kidney
    beans, drained

400 g / 14 oz / 1 ¾ cups canned
    sweetcorn, drained

6 tbsp soured cream

salt and black pepper

GARNISH

coriander (cilantro) leaves

- Heat the oil in a large frying pan and fry the
  onion, pepper and chilli for 10 minutes, stirring
  occasionally. Add the garlic and cayenne and cook
  for 2 minutes, then add the mince.

- Fry the mince until it starts to brown then scrape
  the mixture into a slow cooker and add the
  tomatoes, stock, beans and sweetcorn.

- Cover the slow cooker and cook on medium for
  5 hours.

- Season with salt and pepper to taste, then ladle into
  warm bowls and top each one with 1 tbsp of soured
  cream and a sprinkle of cayenne. Garnish with
  coriander before serving.

SERVES

4

Beef and stout stew

PREPARATION TIME: 35 MINUTES | COOKING TIME: 6 HOURS

INGREDIENTS

450 g / 1 lb / 3 cups chuck steak, cut
   into large chunks
4 tbsp plain (all purpose) flour
2 tbsp butter
1 onion, finely chopped
1 celery stick, finely chopped
3 cloves of garlic, chopped
1 tbsp Dijon mustard
2 bay leaves
1 tbsp Worcestershire sauce
700 ml / 1 pint 3 ½ fl. oz / 2 ¾ cups
   stout
chips and salad skewers to serve
salt and black pepper

- Season the beef with salt and pepper and dust the pieces with flour to coat. Heat the butter in a large frying pan and sear the beef in batches on all sides.

- Transfer the beef to a slow cooker, then add the onion and celery to the frying pan and cook without colouring for 5 minutes.

- Add the garlic, mustard and bay leaves and cook for 1 more minute. Pour in the stout and bring to the boil, then tip everything into the slow cooker.

- Put the lid on the slow cooker and cook on low for 6 hours, stirring every 2 hours.

- Pass the sauce through a colander into a wide saucepan and reduce on the hob until very thick. Season to taste with salt and pepper.

- Stir the beef back into the sauce and serve with chips and salad skewers.

SERVES

Chicken and turnip stew

PREPARATION TIME: 10 MINUTES | COOKING TIME: 4 HOURS

INGREDIENTS

2 tbsp olive oil

450 g / 1 lb / 2 cups chicken breast,
    sliced

1 red onion, sliced

2 cloves of garlic, finely chopped

400 g / 14 oz / 2 cups baby turnips,
    scrubbed

600 ml / 1 pint / 2 ½ cups chicken
    stock

1 tbsp Dijon mustard

salt and black pepper

- Heat the oil in a frying pan and sear the chicken pieces all over. Transfer the chicken to a slow cooker with a slotted spoon.

- Stir the rest of the ingredients into the slow cooker, then cover with a lid and cook on low for 4 hours.

- Season to taste with salt and pepper before serving.

SERVES

6

Beef and vegetable ragu

PREPARATION TIME: **15 MINUTES** | COOKING TIME: **5 HOURS**

INGREDIENTS

3 tbsp olive oil
1 onion, finely chopped
4 cloves of garlic, crushed
450 g / 1 lb / 3 cups minced beef
2 tbsp concentrated tomato puree
200 ml / 7 fl. oz / ¾ cup red wine
½ butternut squash, peeled and diced
2 courgettes (zucchini), diced
1 aubergine (eggplant), diced
400 ml / 14 fl. oz / 1 ½ cups beef stock
2 tbsp basil leaves, chopped
spaghetti to serve
salt and black pepper

- Heat the oil in a large frying pan and fry the onion and garlic for 5 minutes, stirring occasionally. Add the mince and fry until it starts to brown then stir in the tomato puree.

- Pour in the wine and boil rapidly for 2 minutes, then scrape everything into a slow cooker and stir in the rest of the ingredients, except for the basil.

- Cover the slow cooker and cook on medium for 5 hours.

- Season with salt and pepper to taste, then stir in the basil and serve with spaghetti.

SERVES

4

Chicken and vegetable stew

PREPARATION TIME: 20 MINUTES | COOKING TIME: 4 HOURS

INGREDIENTS

2 tbsp olive oil

450 g / 1 lb / 2 cups chicken breast, cubed

1 leek, sliced

1 celery stick, diced

2 cloves of garlic, crushed

400 g / 14 oz / 2 cups canned tomatoes, chopped

600 ml / 1 pint / 2 ½ cups chicken stock

1 lemon, juiced and zest finely grated

salt and black pepper

GARNISH

2 tbsp flat leaf parsley, chopped

- Heat the oil in a frying pan and sear the chicken pieces all over. Transfer the chicken to a slow cooker with a slotted spoon.

- Add the leek, celery and garlic to the frying pan and cook without colouring for 5 minutes. Pour in the tomatoes and stock and bring to the boil, then pour it over the chicken.

- Cover the slow cooker and cook on low for 4 hours.

- Stir the lemon juice and zest into the stew and season with salt and pepper to taste. Sprinkle over the parsley and serve immediately.

SERVES

4

Lamb stew with spring vegetables

PREPARATION TIME: 20 MINUTES | COOKING TIME: 5 HOURS 30 MINUTES

INGREDIENTS

4 thick slices lamb neck, on the bone
2 tbsp plain (all purpose) flour
2 tbsp olive oil
125 ml / 4 ½ fl. oz / ½ cup white wine
12 new potatoes, scrubbed
2 leeks, cut into chunks
12 baby carrots, scrubbed
500 ml / 17 ½ fl. oz / 2 cups good
    quality lamb stock
4 runner beans, halved and sliced
    lengthways
2 tbsp kalamata olives
salt and black pepper

GARNISH

flat leaf parsley

- Preheat the oven to 160°C (140°C fan) / 325F / gas 3.

- Season the lamb with salt and pepper and dust with flour to coat. Heat the oil in a large frying pan and sear the lamb on all sides.

- Transfer the lamb to a slow cooker, then deglaze the pan with the wine and scrape it in with the lamb. Add the potatoes, leeks, carrots and stock to the slow cooker and season well with salt and pepper.

- Put the lid on the slow cooker and cook on low for 5 hours. Stir in the beans and olives, then cover and cook for another 30 minutes. Serve garnished with parsley.

SERVES

6

Slow-cooked seafood, bacon and bean stew

PREPARATION TIME: 15 MINUTES | COOKING TIME: 6 HOURS 30 MINUTES

INGREDIENTS

300 g / 10 ½ oz / 2 cups haricot beans,
    soaked overnight
225 g / 8 oz piece boiling bacon,
    cut into lardons
1 leek, chopped
1 carrot, chopped
a pinch of saffron
600 ml / 1 pint / 2 ½ cups live mussels,
    scrubbed
300 g / 10 ½ oz / 1 cup queen scallops
    (shelled weight)
200 ml / 7 fl. oz / ¾ cup double
    (heavy) cream
2 tbsp basil, shredded

- Drain the beans of their soaking water, then tip them into a saucepan, cover with cold water and bring to the boil. Cook for 10 minutes then drain well.

- Tip the beans into a slow cooker and stir in the bacon, leek, carrot, saffron and 1 litre of water. Cover and cook on medium for 6 hours.

- Stir in the mussels, scallops and cream, then cover again and cook for a further 30 minutes or until all of the mussels have opened.

- Taste the sauce for seasoning and adjust with salt and pepper. Pick out most of the mussel meat and discard the shells, leaving a few on for decoration.

- Ladle into warm bowls and serve garnished with basil.

PUDDINGS

SERVES

6

Stewed summer berries

PREPARATION TIME: **5 MINUTES** | COOKING TIME: **2 HOURS**

INGREDIENTS

150 g / 5 ½ oz / 1 cup raspberries
150 g / 5 ½ oz / 1 cup blackberries
150 g / 5 ½ oz / 1 cup redcurrants
150 g / 5 ½ oz / 1 cup wild
   strawberries
4 tbsp caster (superfine) sugar
4 tbsp crème de cassis

- Mix everything together in a small slow cooker, then cover and cook on low for 2 hours.

- Serve warm from the pot or transfer to a serving bowl and chill in the fridge.

SERVES

6

Apples and pears with vanilla syrup

PREPARATION TIME: 25 MINUTES | COOKING TIME: 2 HOURS

INGREDIENTS

6 eating apples, peeled and halved
6 pears, peeled and halved
1 lemon, juiced
6 tbsp caster (superfine) sugar
2 vanilla pods, split lengthways

- Mix all of the ingredients together in a slow cooker and pour over enough boiling water to come halfway up the side of the fruit. Top with a crumpled layer of greaseproof paper, then put on the lid and cook on medium for 2 hours.

- Transfer the fruit to a warm serving bowl. Scrape out the vanilla seeds and stir them into the cooking liquid, then discard the pods.

- Transfer the cooking liquid to a saucepan and boil until reduced to a shiny syrup. Spoon the syrup over the fruit and serve warm or chilled.

SERVES

6

Spiced rhubarb

PREPARATION TIME: 45 MINUTES | COOKING TIME: 2 HOURS

INGREDIENTS

800 g / 1 lb 12 ½ oz rhubarb stalks
2 star anise
6 cardamom pods
150 g / 5 ½ oz / ⅔ cup caster
   (superfine) sugar

- Cut the rhubarb into short lengths and put it in a slow cooker with the spices.

- Sprinkle over the sugar and 3 tbsp of water, then cover and cook on medium for 2 hours.

- Serve warm or leave to cool completely before chilling in the fridge.

SERVES

4

Salted caramel apples

PREPARATION TIME: 10 MINUTES | COOKING TIME: 1 HOUR

INGREDIENTS

4 small Bramley apples
4 tbsp salted butter
4 tbsp light brown sugar

- Preheat the oven to 160°C (140°C fan) / 325F / gas 3.

- Use an apple corer to remove the apple cores, then sit them in a snug baking dish. Cream the butter and sugar together then pack the mixture into the cavities.

- Bake the apples for 1 hour or until a skewer will slide in easily all the way to the centre.

SERVES

4

Spiced pears in red wine

PREPARATION TIME: 5 MINUTES | COOKING TIME: 2 HOURS

INGREDIENTS

8 small pears, peeled and cored
4 tbsp caster (superfine) sugar
500 ml / 17 ½ fl. oz / 2 cups red wine
6 cloves
2 cinnamon sticks
2 bay leaves

- Put everything in a slow cooker, then cover and cook on medium for 2 hours, turning the pears half way through.

- Serve warm or chilled.

SERVES

6

Cinnamon apple compote

PREPARATION TIME: 5 MINUTES | COOKING TIME: 2 HOURS

INGREDIENTS

2 bramley apples, peeled, cored and
  diced
8 eating apples, peeled, cored and
  diced
1 lemon, juiced
150 ml / 5 ½ fl. oz / ⅔ cup apple juice
4 tbsp caster (superfine) sugar
2 cinnamon sticks

- Mix all of the ingredients together in a slow cooker, then put on the lid and cook on low for 2 hours.

- Spoon the compote into sterilised jars and seal whilst still hot.

SERVES

6

Red fruits with nuts and cream

PREPARATION TIME: 25 MINUTES | COOKING TIME: 2 HOURS

INGREDIENTS

150 g / 5 ½ oz / 1 cup raspberries
150 g / 5 ½ oz / 1 cup cranberries
150 g / 5 ½ oz / 1 cup redcurrants
150 g / 5 ½ oz / 1 cup cherries
75 g / 2 ½ oz / ⅓ cup caster
  (superfine) sugar
4 tbsp cherry brandy
300 ml / 10 ½ fl. oz / 1 ¼ cups double
  (heavy) cream
50 g / 1 ¾ oz / ⅔ cup toasted flaked
  (slivered) almonds, chopped

- Mix the fruit with the sugar and brandy in a small slow cooker, then cover and cook on low for 2 hours.

- Leave to cool to room temperature, then chill in the fridge until you're ready to serve.

- Whip the cream until it holds its shape, then spoon it into a piping bag fitted with a large star nozzle.

- Divide the berries between 6 dessert glasses and sprinkle with the almonds. Pipe a swirl on cream on top of each one and serve immediately.

SERVES

4

Slow-roasted fruit salad

PREPARATION TIME: 10 MINUTES | COOKING TIME: 1 HOUR

INGREDIENTS

3 tbsp butter

3 eating apples, cored and cut into
   wedges

3 pears, cored and cut into wedges

a few sprigs of thyme

2 ruby grapefruit

2 tbsp caster (superfine) sugar

black pepper

- Preheat the oven to 160°C (140°C fan) / 325F / gas 3.

- Put the butter in a roasting tin and put it in the oven
  to melt for 2 minutes.

- Carefully toss the apples, pears and thyme in the
  butter and season with black pepper. Transfer the
  dish to the oven and roast for 30 minutes.

- Meanwhile, slice the top and bottom off the
  grapefruit. Slice away the peel then cut out each
  individual segment, leaving the white pith behind
  and collecting any juices in a bowl. Discard the pith.

- Stir the grapefruit segments and juices into the
  roasting tin, then return to the oven for a further
  30 minutes.

SERVES

6

Vanilla poached cherries

PREPARATION TIME: 10 MINUTES | COOKING TIME: 1 HOUR 30 MINUTES

INGREDIENTS

900 g / 2 lb / 5 cups black cherries,
   stoned
100 g / 3 ½ oz / ½ cup caster
   (superfine) sugar
100 ml / 3 ½ fl. oz / ½ cup rosé wine
1 vanilla pod, split lengthways
3 tbsp kirsch
vanilla ice cream to serve

- Mix the cherries with the sugar, wine and vanilla pod in a slow cooker. Cover and cook on medium for 1 hour 30 minutes then stir in the kirsch and leave to cool.

- Discard the vanilla pod, then spoon the cherries and their cooking liquor into bowls and serve with vanilla ice cream.

SERVES

8

Slow-cooked pears and rhubarb

PREPARATION TIME: **10 MINUTES** | COOKING TIME: **3 HOURS**

INGREDIENTS

800 g / 1 lb 12 ½ oz rhubarb stalks
150 g / 5 ½ oz / ⅔ cup caster
  (superfine) sugar
6 pears, peeled, cored and chopped

- Cut the rhubarb into short lengths and toss it with the sugar. Tip it into one side of a slow cooker and tip the pears into the other side.

- Sprinkle over 3 tbsp of water, then cover and cook on medium for 3 hours.

- Serve warm from the pot or transfer to a serving bowl and chill in the fridge.

SERVES

4

Slow-baked cinnamon apples

PREPARATION TIME: **10 MINUTES** | COOKING TIME: **1 HOUR**

INGREDIENTS

4 small Bramley apples
3 tbsp butter, melted
2 tbsp caster (superfine) sugar
1 tsp ground cinnamon
4 scoops vanilla ice cream

- Preheat the oven to 160°C (140°C fan) / 325F / gas 3.

- Score a ring around the middle of each apple with a sharp knife then sit them in a snug baking dish and brush with melted butter. Mix the sugar with the cinnamon and sprinkle it over the top.

- Bake the apples for 1 hour or until a skewer will slide in easily all the way to the centre.

- Cut each apple in half horizontally, then top with a scoop of ice cream and sandwich back together. Serve immediately.

SERVES

6

Poires belle helene

PREPARATION TIME: 25 MINUTES | COOKING TIME: 2 HOURS

INGREDIENTS

3 tbsp caster (superfine) sugar
500 ml / 17 ½ fl. oz / 2 cups perry
  (pear cider)
6 pears, peeled and cored
200 g / 7 oz / 1 cup dark chocolate
  (minimum 60% cocoa solids)
150 ml / 5 ½ fl. oz / ⅔ cup double
  (heavy) cream
2 tbsp Poire William liqueur
good quality vanilla ice cream to serve

- Stir the sugar into the perry in a small slow cooker to dissolve, then add the pears and cover with a crumpled piece of greaseproof paper.

- Cover and cook on medium for 2 hours, turning the pears half way through. Leave in the cooking liquid to cool to room temperature.

- Chop the chocolate and transfer it to a small saucepan with the cream and liqueur. Stir it over a gentle heat until the chocolate melts and the sauce is smooth and shiny.

- Divide the pears between 6 bowls and spoon over the warm chocolate sauce. Serve with vanilla ice cream.

SERVES

4

Mini casseroles of pear and cinnamon

PREPARATION TIME: **10 MINUTES** | COOKING TIME: **2 HOURS**

INGREDIENTS

4 pears, peeled, cored and halved
4 cinnamon sticks, halved
4 tbsp honey
4 tbsp Poire William liqueur

- Preheat the oven to 150°C (130°C fan) / 300F / gas 2.

- Arrange the pear halves and cinnamon sticks in 4 individual casserole dishes. Drizzle over the honey and liqueur.

- Put the lids on the dishes and transfer them to the oven. Bake for 2 hours or until the pears are really tender.

199

SERVES

4

Poached apples with sesame caramel

PREPARATION TIME: **30 MINUTES** | COOKING TIME: **1 HOUR 30 MINUTES**

INGREDIENTS

4 apples, peeled, cored and halved
500 ml / 17 ½ fl. oz / 2 cups apple juice
1 tbsp butter
1 tsp sesame oil
½ tbsp sesame seeds

- Arrange the apples cut side down in a single layer in a slow cooker. Pour over the apple juice then cook on medium for 1 hour 30 minutes or until the apples are tender to the point of a knife.

- Drain the apples through a colander and collect the juice in a saucepan. Boil the juice over a high heat until it has reduced to a syrupy consistency, then whisk in the butter and sesame oil to make a shiny caramel sauce.

- Divide the apples between 4 bowls, then drizzle over the sauce and sprinkle with sesame seeds.

SERVES

4

Poached peaches
with saffron

PREPARATION TIME: 30 MINUTES | COOKING TIME: 1 HOUR 30 MINUTES

INGREDIENTS

6 peaches, halved and stoned
100 g / 3 ½ oz / ½ cup caster
    (superfine) sugar
1 lemon
a pinch of saffron

- Put the peaches in a slow cooker with the sugar and 200 ml / 7 fl. oz / ¾ cup of water.

- Use a vegetable peeler to remove the lemon rind in thin strips and add them to the cooker along with the saffron. Stir well.

- Cover and cook on medium for 1 hour 30 minutes or until the peaches are tender, but still holding their shape.

SERVES

6

Knickerbocker glory

PREPARATION TIME: **10 MINUTES** | COOKING TIME: **1 HOUR 30 MINUTES**

INGREDIENTS

1 pineapple, peeled and cut into
  chunks
300 g / 10 ½ oz / 1 ⅔ cups black
  cherries, stoned
3 pears, peeled, cored and cut into
  chunks
100 g / 3 ½ oz / ½ cup caster
  (superfine) sugar
100 ml / 3 ½ fl. oz / ½ cup rosé wine
6 scoops vanilla ice cream
50 g / 1 ¾ oz / ½ cup pistachio nuts,
  chopped

- Mix the fruit with the sugar and wine in a slow cooker. Cover and cook on medium for 1 hour 30 minutes then leave to cool completely.

- Spoon the fruit and cooking liquor into 6 tall sundae glasses and top with the ice cream and pistachio nuts.

BAKES

SERVES

4

Date and apple crumble

PREPARATION TIME: 20 MINUTES | COOKING TIME: 1 HOUR 30 MINUTES

INGREDIENTS

4 eating apples, peeled, cored and
   diced
1 large bramley apple, peeled, cored
   and diced
2 tbsp muscovado sugar
150 g / 5 ½ oz / ⅔ cup medjool dates,
   stoned and chopped
1 tsp ground mixed spice
75 g / 2 ½ oz / ⅓ cup butter
100 g / 3 ½ oz / ⅔ cup plain (all
   purpose) flour
25 g / 1 oz / ¼ cup ground almonds
40 g / 1 ½ oz / ¼ cup light brown sugar

- Preheat the oven to 160°C (140°C fan) / 325F / gas 3.

- Mix the apples with the muscovado sugar and 4 tbsp of water in a baking dish. Cover the dish with foil and bake in the oven for 1 hour.

- Take the fruit out of the oven, stir in the dates and mixed spice and increase the temperature to 180°C (160°C fan) / 350F / gas 4.

- Rub the butter into the flour and stir in the ground almonds and sugar. Take a handful of the topping and squeeze it into a clump, then crumble it over the fruit. Repeat with the rest of the crumble mixture then bake for 30 minutes or until the topping is golden brown.

SERVES

4

Plum and cocoa clafoutis

PREPARATION TIME: 20 MINUTES | COOKING TIME: 1 HOUR 30 MINUTES

INGREDIENTS

75 g / 2 ½ oz / ⅓ cup caster (superfine)
   sugar
75 g / 2 ½ oz / ⅓ cup butter
300 ml / 10 ½ fl. oz / 1 ¼ cups whole
   milk
2 large eggs
50 g / 1 ¾ oz / ⅓ cup plain (all
   purpose) flour
1 tbsp unsweetened cocoa powder
4 plums, halved and stoned
icing (confectioners') sugar to dust

- Preheat the oven to 190°C (170°C fan) / 375F / gas 5.

- Melt the butter in a saucepan and cook over a low heat until it starts to smell nutty. Brush a little of the butter around the inside of a baking dish then add a spoonful of caster sugar and shake to coat.

- Whisk together the milk and eggs with the rest of the butter. Sift the flour and cocoa into a mixing bowl with a pinch of salt, then stir in the rest of the sugar. Make a well in the middle of the dry ingredients and gradually whisk in the liquid, incorporating all the flour from round the outside until you have a lump-free batter.

- Pour the batter into the baking dish and top with the plum halves.

- Bake the clafoutis for 15 minutes, then reduce the oven temperature to 160°C (140°C fan) / 325F / gas 3. Cook for a further 1 hour 15 minutes or until the centre is set with just a slight wobble. Serve warm or chilled dusted with icing sugar.

SERVES

6

Apricot and pistachio clafoutis

PREPARATION TIME: 20 MINUTES | COOKING TIME: 1 HOUR 30 MINUTES

INGREDIENTS

75 g / 2 ½ oz / ⅓ cup caster (superfine) sugar

75 g / 2 ½ oz / ⅓ cup butter

300 ml / 10 ½ fl. oz / 1 ¼ cups whole milk

2 large eggs

1 lemon, zest finely grated

50 g / 1 ¾ oz / ⅓ cup plain (all purpose) flour

400 g / 14 oz / 1 ½ cups canned apricot halves, drained

3 tbsp pistachio nuts, chopped

- Preheat the oven to 190°C (170°C fan) / 375F / gas 5.

- Melt the butter in a saucepan and cook over a low heat until it starts to smell nutty. Brush a little of the butter around the inside of a baking dish then add a spoonful of caster sugar and shake to coat.

- Whisk together the milk and eggs with the lemon zest and the rest of the butter. Sift the flour into a mixing bowl with a pinch of salt, then stir in the rest of the sugar. Make a well in the middle of the dry ingredients and gradually whisk in the liquid, incorporating all the flour from round the outside until you have a lump-free batter.

- Pour the batter into the baking dish and top with the apricot halves and pistachios.

- Bake the clafoutis for 15 minutes, then reduce the oven temperature to 160°C (140°C fan) / 325F / gas 3. Cook for a further 1 hour 15 minutes or until the centre is set with just a slight wobble. Serve warm or chilled.

SERVES

Crème caramel

PREPARATION TIME: 20 MINUTES | COOKING TIME: 3 HOURS | CHILLING TIME: 4 HOURS

INGREDIENTS

175 g / 6 oz / ¾ cup caster (superfine)
   sugar
1 tbsp butter, softened
600 ml / 1 pint / 2 ½ cups whole milk
4 large eggs

- Preheat the slow cooker to low.

- Put 150 g of the sugar in a heavy-based saucepan and heat gently until it starts to turn liquid at the edges. Continue to heat and swirl the pan until the sugar has all melted and turned golden brown. Divide the caramel between 6 small glass dishes and leave to set, then butter the sides of the dishes.

- Whisk the milk and eggs with the remaining 25 g of sugar and divide between the ramekins. Cover each ramekin with buttered foil. Sit the ramekins in the slow cooker and pour enough boiling water around them to come halfway up the sides.

- Cook on low for 3 hours or until the crème caramels are just set with a slight wobble in the centre. Remove the ramekins from the tray and chill for 4 hours or overnight.

SERVES

4

Gingerbread-stuffed baked apples

PREPARATION TIME: **10 MINUTES** | COOKING TIME: **1 HOUR**

INGREDIENTS

4 eating apples
100 g / 3 ½ oz / 1 cup ginger cake,
   crumbled
2 tbsp butter, melted
50 g / 1 ¾ oz / ½ cup almonds, chopped
2 tbsp runny honey

- Preheat the oven to 160°C (140°C fan) / 325F / gas 3.
- Cut the apples in half and use a melon baller to remove the cores.
- Mix the cake crumbs with the butter and almonds, then pack the mixture into the cavities.
- Bake the apples for 1 hour or until a skewer will slide in easily all the way to the centre.
- Serve drizzled with honey.

SERVES

6

Orange crème caramel

PREPARATION TIME: **20 MINUTES** | COOKING TIME: **3 HOURS** | CHILLING TIME: **4 HOURS**

INGREDIENTS

175 g / 6 oz / ¾ cup caster (superfine)
    sugar
1 tbsp butter, softened
500 ml / 17 ½ fl. oz / 2 cups whole milk
100 ml / 3 ½ fl. oz / ½ cup orange juice,
    sieved
4 large eggs
1 tsp orange zest, finely grated
1 tbsp orange liqueur

- Preheat the slow cooker to low.

- Put 150 g of the sugar in a heavy-based saucepan and heat gently until it starts to turn liquid at the edges. Continue to heat and swirl the pan until the sugar has all melted and turned golden brown. Divide the caramel between 6 ramekin dishes and leave to set, then butter the sides of the ramekins.

- Whisk the rest of the ingredients with the remaining 25 g of sugar and divide between the ramekins. Cover each ramekin with buttered foil. Sit the ramekins in the slow cooker and pour enough boiling water around them to come halfway up the sides.

- Cook on low for 3 hours or until the crème caramels are just set with a slight wobble in the centre. Remove the ramekins from the tray and chill for 4 hours or overnight.

- Give the ramekins a vigorous shake to loosen the crème caramels, then turn each one out onto a plate.

Index

Apples and pears with vanilla syrup, 176

Apricot and pistachio clafoutis, 212

Bean and buckwheat broth, 32

Beef and stout stew, 160

Beef and vegetable ragu, 164

Beef in coconut milk, 56

Beef in red wine with shallots, 46

Beef shin with carrots, 58

Beef, chorizo and mushroom stew, 142

Beef, turnip and lardon stew, 154

Boeuf bourguignon, 124

Braised oxtail with chorizo and turnip, 66

Carrot and squash soup, 20

Chicken and barley broth, 16

Chicken and butternut Colombo, 42

Chicken and celeriac stew, 30

Chicken and preserved lemon tagine, 128

Chicken and turnip stew, 162

Chicken and vegetable stew, 166

Chicken and vegetables with cashew nuts, 144

Chicken blanquette, 76

Chicken curry, 80

Chicken leg curry, 68

Chicken legs with chickpeas and chorizo, 84

Chicken with chanterelles, 74

Chicken with figs and broad beans, 78

Chicken with morels, 44

Chicken with mozzarella and herbs, 100

Chicken, potato and bean stew, 140

Chicken, potato and pepper tagine, 136

Chilli con carne, 158

Chorizo and lentil soup, 38

Cinnamon apple compote, 184

Confit peppers with sea bass, 110

Crème caramel, 214

Date and apple crumble, 206

French onion soup, 28

Gingerbread-stuffed baked apples, 216

Hake and potato stew, 152

Ham and bean stew, 138

Ham hock pot au feu, 18

Ham pot au feu, 148

Japanese prawn and noodle soup, 22

Knickerbocker glory, 204

Lamb chops with tomato sauce, 102

Lamb stew with spring vegetables, 168

Leek, potato and bacon soup with pesto, 34

Meatballs in tomato sauce, 94

Mini casseroles of pear and cinnamon, 198

Mixed pulse stew, 130

Monkfish with mango and coconut milk, 114

Mushroom soup, 24

Orange crème caramel, 218

Ox cheek and stout stew, 156

Paupiettes of veal with tomato sauce, 86

Pike perch with sorrel sauce, 112

Plum and coca clafoutis, 210

Poached apples with sesame caramel, 200

Poached beef with ginger, 92

Poached chicken with spices, 14

Poached peaches with saffron, 202

Poached salmon with vegetable julienne, 106

Poached topside with vegetables, 72

Poires belle helene, 196

Pork and aubergine Colombo, 64

Pork and peach stew, 126

Pot-roasted cod with fennel stems, 108

Pot-roasted paupiettes of pork with carrots, 62

Pot-roasted paupiettes of veal with baby onions, 48

Pot-roasted paupiettes of veal, 54

Prawn and rice noodle broth, 26

Red fruits with nuts and cream, 186

Salmon and vegetable stew, 120

Salted caramel apples, 180

Sea bass paupiettes, 116

Seafood and vegetable stew, 122

Seafood ragu, 12

Shellfish chowder, 132

Slow-baked cinnamon apples, 194

Slow-baked Spanish chicken, 50

Slow-cooked beef in red wine with carrots, 96

Slow-cooked beef with mushrooms, 90

Slow-cooked brisket pot au feu, 146

Slow-cooked pears and rhubarb, 192

Slow-cooked seafood, bacon and bean stew, 170

Slow-cooked turkey blanquette, 98

Slow-roasted brisket with tomatoes, 88

Slow-roasted fillet steaks with shallots and garlic, 82

Slow-roasted fruit salad, 188

Slow-roasted hangar steak with salsa, 60

Slow-roasted sirloin steak with fig sauce, 52

Spiced pears in red wine, 182

Spiced rhubarb, 178

Squash and apple soup, 36

Stewed peppers and tomatoes, 150

Stewed summer berries, 174

Thai green meatball curry, 70

Vanilla poached cherries, 190

Vegetarian hot pot, 134